The Mind of Robert Louis Stevenson

Selected Essays, Letters, and Prayers

The Mind of
Robert Louis Stevenson

Selected Essays, Letters, and Prayers

Edited by
Roger Ricklefs

Essay Index Reprint Series

BOOKS FOR LIBRARIES PRESS
FREEPORT, NEW YORK

STANDARD BOOK NUMBER:

8369-1430-9

LIBRARY OF CONGRESS CATALOG CARD NUMBER:

72-99651

PRINTED IN THE UNITED STATES OF AMERICA

Acknowledgments

The editor gratefully acknowledges the expert aid in many research matters of the Widener Library at Harvard University. The assistance of Mrs. Sheila Kravetz, who typed the manuscript with meticulous care, is also greatly appreciated.

For invaluable instruction and advice, the editor is grateful to the Robert Louis Stevenson School faculty, and particularly to Mrs. Sybil Bolitho Fearnley, Instructor of English. Without her instruction for five years and her guidance for over a decade, this book would have been impossible. For encouragement and guidance, the editor will always be indebted to his parents. By example, they set a high standard for both of their sons and for all of their students.

The letter to Mrs. Stevenson is used by permission of Charles Scribner's Sons, from *The Letters of Robert Louis Stevenson to His Family and Friends*. Selected and edited by Sidney Colvin. Volume I, Biographical Edition; Copyright 1907 Charles Scribner's Sons; renewal copyright 1935 Lloyd Osbourne.

Contents

Introduction

Can a good man be interesting?

No, the novelists and biographers seem to say, for frequently their most fascinating characters are their worst. Long after the reader forgets Benjamin Franklin and the pennies saved, he remembers Adolf Hitler and the corpses of Buchenwald.

Robert Louis Stevenson, however, proves that the good man can be compellingly fascinating, both as an author and as an individual. Stevenson's courage and compassion are even part of his fascination, part of the legend which has developed around him.

The legend portrays Stevenson as a courageous invalid who led an active and adventurous life; as a man who struggled for subsistence and finally won sensational success; as a friend of the poor and a crusader for social justice.

And for all its exaggeration, the legend is based on truth. It is merely incomplete. This book will therefore not refute the legend; it will go beyond it. Through the author's own words, it will portray the wide range of his traits and moods: humor, anger, toleration, indignation, youthful atheism, later piety, profundity and, refreshingly enough in a famous man, occasional uninhibited silliness.

But if these writings derive diversity from their author's complex mind, they gain unity from the constant originality and brilliance of his style. For individually, these works are among the best of Stevenson's nonfiction. Collectively, they portray Stevenson's most fascinating character—himself.

9

To understand this character and his writing, one needs at least a brief biographical sketch. In many cases, the correlation between the life and the work is nebulous; in Stevenson's case, it is significant and direct.

Stevenson was born in 1850 in Edinburgh, Scotland, the son of a brilliant, successful, orthodox, Calvinist and bigoted civil engineer. The boy soon showed a love for learning and a hatred for uninspired pedagogy.

He also showed literary talent. As he recollects, "I kept always two books in my pocket, one to read, one to write in." At the age of sixteen, the energetic author published his first book, a short account of a revolt in 1666. His father proudly financed the work. The energy and discipline which produced a book at this early age were never lost. Stevenson wrote the final version of *Dr. Jekyll and Mr. Hyde* in six days. In the last four years of his life, he wrote 700,000 published words.

The father's early pride in Stevenson's achievements soon gave way to intense dissatisfaction with his ideas. As is characteristic of his independence, Stevenson refused to accept all of his era's religious orthodoxy. Unlike many young men, Stevenson did not embrace atheism with triumphant pride. He was intellectually forced into it. Knowing that his decision would split him from his father, he chose to accept atheism rather than to live what he then considered a lie. Some of the early Stevenson letters included in this book reveal the author's painful struggle between loyalty to his family and loyalty to his conception of the truth. Stevenson later changed his religious views. His prayers have the sincerity, the conviction, and the power possible only to the man who has struggled for his own answer.

To complicate his early family struggles, Stevenson had no taste for the "family profession," civil engineering. Disgusting as it sounded to the Victorian parents, he wanted to write.

Finally forced to realize that their son would never design bridges, the parents settled for his becoming a lawyer. Stevenson forced himself to study law and was finally admitted to the bar. During his brief career in law, he spent too much of his money on poor friends and too little of his time reading law books. He had a very small practice.

As this offered him ample time to write, literature gained from Stevenson's legal mediocrity. The *Cornhill* and *London* magazines now published Stevenson's essays and stories fairly regularly. Although his ability was slowly gaining recognition, Stevenson still suffered emotionally from a violent family split and physically from seemingly chronic sickness.

The series of illnesses often forced him to leave Scotland for a warmer climate. During one trip to France, he met Mrs. Fanny Osbourne, an American about to be divorced. In proper British society, American divorcées were no more fashionable then than they were in Edward VIII's time. But once again, Stevenson decided to risk family condemnation. Traveling in squalid poverty, he followed Mrs. Osbourne to California where she awaited her divorce. During this period, he lived in Monterey, California, and survived on newspaper work. In 1880, nearing death from tuberculosis and lacking both present funds and future prospects, Stevenson married Mrs. Osbourne. They subsisted briefly in San Francisco and Calistoga, California.

The couple returned to Scotland. As the bond of affection had never been permanently broken, Stevenson and his family achieved reconciliation. Through the use of charm and common sense, Fanny won the family approval.

Moreover, Stevenson soon emerged as a major literary figure. In 1883, *Treasure Island* appeared in book form and attracted public attention. After *Dr. Jekyll and Mr. Hyde* was published in 1886, Stevenson's success was assured. Preachers around the world discussed the book's moral implications; this was as valuable as a television plug is today. As the final proof of Stevenson's arrival, the words "Jekyll and Hyde" became a household expression. When Stevenson returned to the United States in 1887, he was sensationally popular. The two tugboats which steered his ship into the New York harbor were called the *Jekyll* and the *Hyde*.

But Stevenson avoided the snobbery of new success. For example, he said that the hundred pounds he was offered for *Treasure Island* were "a slight more than *Treasure Island* is worth." Measured in monetary value alone, this volume has made fortunes for its various publishers.

In 1888, still searching for a climate which would help his health, Stevenson, his wife, and her son Lloyd sailed for the South Seas. In Hawaii, Stevenson developed a strong interest in the leper colony where Father Damien served. He spent a week there. The visit provided the basis for the indignation expressed in "Father Damien, an Open Letter to the Reverend Dr. Hyde of Honolulu."

Stevenson settled permanently in Samoa. Colonial exploitation of natives and disregard for their human dignity soon troubled him deeply. He took into his household natives whom other colonists mistreated.

His relations with the natives made him a combination of feudal lord and crusading reformer. He maintained a huge household which numerous natives kept largely self-sufficient. But the household came from the future as well as the past. In an era of vast social differences, Stevenson treated the natives almost as equals. His wife said: "We don't have servants. We have families. If you called the money you give your family for spending money 'wages,' they'd all leave you in a body." In an era of unashamed, largely unquestioned imperialism, Stevenson denounced colonial abuses. His crusading *Footnote to History* directed public attention to the frequent injustice, scandal, and shame of imperial colonial glory.

Stevenson also helped a group of natives who were unjustly imprisoned. The natives were so grateful that they gave Stevenson an unusual but completely utilitarian gift, namely, a road to his house. This was known as "The Road of the Loving Heart, a free gift to Tusitala, Teller of Tales." A sign read:

The Road of Gratitude

Considering the great love of His Excellency, Tusitala in his loving care of us in tribulation in the prison, we have prepared this splendid gift. It shall never be muddy. It shall endure forever, this road that we have made.

Stevenson gave in return one of his gayest parties. It was also one of his last. On December 3, 1894, he died.

After forty-four turbulent years, he left a literary legacy that honors his energy and discipline as much as his talent. Either alone or in collaboration, he wrote a total of twenty-eight volumes, not counting letters. Most of these books are the product not only of painstaking work, but also of a struggle against illness, family strife, or poverty.

As the author of these works, Stevenson has received eloquent praise from literary critics throughout the world. But as a man, Stevenson received perhaps his greatest tribute from illiterate Samoan natives who had no interest whatsoever in English literature. When Stevenson died, the local natives gathered in a lengthy procession and carried his body up Samoa's Mount Vaea. At the end of the strange ceremony, the native chieftains praised Stevenson. One said simply: "Tusitala is dead. We were in prison and he cared for us. We were hungry and he fed us. We were sick and he made us well. The day was no longer than his kindness."

Stevenson's life sets a standard, particularly for the adventurous, the courageous and the young. It is magnificently appropriate that a boys' preparatory school has been named in his honor.

The traits revealed in Stevenson's life are emphasized in his works. Each piece in this collection develops the character of the author.

The first two essays, "Crabbed Age and Youth" and "Child's Play" enthusiastically defend the young, particularly the adventurous young. Stevenson regarded youth with more affection and less condescension than did almost any other English writer. It was Stevenson who dignified a boy's quest for hidden treasure by making it the subject of a major novel.

The third essay deals with the other extremity of life, old age, and death. But like the essays on youth, "Æs Triplex" renounces the timid existence in favor of the adventurous, full life.

With similar eloquence and vigor, "Father Damien" and the chapter from *A Footnote to History* condemn hypocrisy and colonial abuses. Marked by a concern for justice which becomes almost emotional, they represent Stevenson at his crusading, table-pounding best.

The next two essays, Part I of "Virginibus Puerisque" and "Talks and Talkers" (first paper) reveal an entirely different facet of Stevenson's personality, namely, charm. To many of his fans, this is Stevenson's predominant characteristic; indeed, he could produce it for hours in conversation and for pages in writing. These two essays offer neither great originality nor great profundity of thought. But the charming style makes the ideas *appear* fresh. Stevenson was a stylist, not a philosopher.

The final essay, "The Philosophy of Umbrellas" is included simply because it is funny.

The series of letters does not claim to be a "representative selection." The vast majority of almost any man's letters are dull. The letters included here are among the most fascinating and the most candid. Most reveal the author's thoughts during his domestic and religious crises.

The final outcome of the religious crisis is expressed in the strong conviction of the prayers. These prayers are widely quoted; one has been adapted as the official prayer of the Robert Louis Stevenson School for Boys. In contrast to the youthful turbulence of the letters, the prayers show calm maturity. The ideas are sometimes old and accepted. But the style has simplicity, eloquence, and beauty.

The prayers therefore typify their author. For in this book the reader will find neither a theologian nor a philosopher, but rather a brilliant stylist and a fascinating man.

ROGER RICKLEFS

The Mind of Robert Louis Stevenson

Selected Essays, Letters, and Prayers

I

Crabbed Age and Youth

"You know my mother now and then argues very notably; always very warmly at least. I happen often to differ from her; and we both think so well of our own arguments, that we very seldom are so happy as to convince one another. A pretty common case, I believe, in all vehement debatings. She says, I am *too witty;* Anglicè, *too pert;* I, that she is *too wise;* that is to say, being likewise put into English, *not so young as she has been."*—Miss Howe to Miss Harlowe, *Clarissa,* vol. ii. Letter xiii.

There is a strong feeling in favour of cowardly and prudential proverbs. The sentiments of a man while he is full of ardour and hope are to be received, it is supposed, with some qualification. But when the same person has ignominiously failed and begins to eat up his words, he should be listened to like an oracle. Most of our pocket wisdom is conceived for the use of mediocre people, to discourage them from ambitious attempts, and generally console them in their mediocrity. And since mediocre people constitute the bulk of humanity, this is no doubt very properly so. But it does not follow that the one sort of proposition is any less true than the other, or that Icarus is not to be more praised, and perhaps more envied, than Mr. Samuel Budgett the Successful Merchant. The one is dead, to be sure, while the other is still in his counting-house counting out his money; and doubtless this is a consideration. But we have, on the other hand, some bold and magnanimous sayings

19

common to high races and natures, which set forth the advantagĕ of the losing side, and proclaim it better to be a dead lion than a living dog. It is difficult to fancy how the mediocrities reconcile such sayings with their proverbs. According to the latter, every lad who goes to sea is an egregious ass; never to forget your umbrella through a long life would seem a higher and wiser flight of achievement than to go smiling to the stake; and so long as you are a bit of a coward and inflexible in money matters, you fulfil the whole duty of man.

It is a still more difficult consideration for our average men, that while all their teachers, from Solomon down to Benjamin Franklin and the ungodly Binney, have inculcated the same ideal of manners, caution, and respectability, those characters in history who have most notoriously flown in the face of such precepts are spoken of in hyperbolical terms of praise, and honoured with public monuments in the streets of our commercial centres. This is very bewildering to the moral sense. You have Joan of Arc, who left a humble but honest and reputable livelihood under the eyes of her parents, to go a-colonelling, in the company of rowdy soldiers, against the enemies of France; surely a melancholy example for one's daughters! And then you have Columbus, who may have pioneered America, but, when all is said, was a most imprudent navigator. His life is not the kind of thing one would like to put into the hands of young people; rather, one would do one's utmost to keep it from their knowledge, as a red flag of adventure and disintegrating influence in life. The time would fail me if I were to recite all the big names in history whose exploits are perfectly irrational and even shocking to the business mind. The incongruity is speaking; and I imagine it must engender among the mediocrities a very peculiar attitude towards the nobler and showier sides of national life. They will read of the Charge of Balaclava in much the same spirit as they assist

at a performance of the *Lyons Mail*. Persons of substance take
in the *Times* and sit composedly in pit or boxes according to
the degree of their prosperity in business. As for the generals
who go galloping up and down among bombshells in absurd
cocked hats—as for the actors who raddle their faces and
demean themselves for hire upon the stage—they must belong,
thank God! to a different order of beings, whom we watch as
we watch the clouds careering in the windy bottomless inane,
or read about like characters in ancient and rather fabulous
annals. Our offspring would no more think of copying their
behaviour, let us hope, than of doffing their clothes and painting themselves blue in consequence of certain admissions in
the first chapter of their school history of England.

Discredited as they are in practice, the cowardly proverbs
hold their own in theory; and it is another instance of the same
spirit, that the opinions of old men about life have been
accepted as final. All sorts of allowances are made for the
illusions of youth; and none, or almost none, for the disenchant-
ments of age. It is held to be a good taunt, and somehow or
other to clinch the question logically, when an old gentleman
waggles his head and says: "Ah, so I thought when I was your
age." It is not thought an answer at all, if the young man
retorts: "My venerable sir, so I shall most probably think when
I am yours." And yet the one is as good as the other: pass for
pass, tit for tat, a Roland for an Oliver.

"Opinion in good men," says Milton, "is but knowledge in
the making." All opinions, properly so called, are stages on the
road to truth. It does not follow that a man will travel any
further; but if he has really considered the world and drawn a
conclusion, he has travelled as far. This does not apply to
formulae got by rote, which are stages on the road to nowhere
but second childhood and the grave. To have a catchword in
your mouth is not the same thing as to hold an opinion; still

less is it the same thing as to have made one for yourself. There are too many of these catchwords in the world for people to rap out upon you like an oath and by way of an argument. They have a currency as intellectual counters; and many respectable persons pay their way with nothing else. They seem to stand for vague bodies of theory in the background. The imputed virtue of folios full of knockdown arguments is supposed to reside in them, just as some of the majesty of the British Empire dwells in the constable's truncheon. They are used in pure superstition, as old clodhoppers spoil Latin by way of an exorcism. And yet they are vastly serviceable for checking unprofitable discussion and stopping the mouths of babes and sucklings. And when a young man comes to a certain stage of intellectual growth, the examination of these counters forms a gymnastic at once amusing and fortifying to the mind.

Because I have reached Paris, I am not ashamed of having passed through Newhaven and Dieppe. They were very good places to pass through, and I am none the less at my destination. All my old opinions were only stages on the way to the one I now hold, as itself is only a stage on the way to something else. I am no more abashed at having been a red-hot Socialist with a panacea of my own than at having been a sucking infant. Doubtless the world is quite right in a million ways; but you have to be kicked about a little to convince you of the fact. And in the meanwhile you must do something, be something, believe something. It is not possible to keep the mind in a state of accurate balance and blank; and even if you could do so, instead of coming ultimately to the right conclusion, you would be very apt to remain in a state of balance and blank to perpetuity. Even in quite intermediate stages, a dash of enthusiasm is not a thing to be ashamed of in the retrospect: if St. Paul had not been a very zealous Pharisee, he would have been a colder Christian. For my part, I look back to the time when I was a Socialist with something like regret. I have convinced myself (for the moment) that we had better leave these great changes to what we call blind forces; their blindness being so much more perspicacious than the little, peering, partial eyesight of men. I seem to see that my own scheme would not answer; and all the other schemes I ever heard propounded would depress some elements of goodness just as much as they encouraged others. Now I know that in thus turning Conservative with years, I am going through the normal cycle of change and travelling in the common orbit of men's opinions. I submit to this, as I would submit to gout or grey hair, as a concomitant of growing age or else of failing animal heat; but I do not acknowledge that it is necessarily a change for the better—I daresay it is deplorably for the worse. I have no choice in the business, and can no more resist this tendency of my mind than I could prevent my body from beginning to totter and decay. If I am spared (as the phrase runs) I shall doubtless outlive some troublesome desires; but I am in no hurry about that; nor, when the time comes, shall I plume myself on the immunity. Just in the same way, I do not greatly pride myself on having outlived my belief in the fairy tales of Socialism. Old people have faults of their own; they tend to become cowardly, niggardly, and suspicious. Whether from the growth of experience or the decline of animal heat, I see that age leads to these and certain other faults; and it follows, of course, that while in one sense I hope I am journeying towards the truth, in another I am indubitably posting towards these forms and sources of error.

As we go catching and catching at this or that corner of knowledge, now getting a foresight of generous possibilities, now chilled with a glimpse of prudence, we may compare the headlong course of our years to a swift torrent in which a man is carried away; now he is dashed against a boulder, now he grapples for a moment to a trailing spray; at the end, he is hurled out and overwhelmed in a dark and bottomless ocean. We have no more than glimpses and touches: we are torn away from our theories; we are spun round and round and shown this or the other view of life, until only fools or knaves can hold to their opinions. We take a sight at a condition in life, and say we have studied it; our most elaborate view is no more than an impression. If we had breathing space, we should take the occasion to modify and adjust; but at this breakneck hurry, we are no sooner boys than we are adult, no sooner in love than married or jilted, no sooner one age than we begin to be another, and no sooner in the fulness of our manhood than we begin to decline towards the grave. It is in vain to seek for consistency or expect clear and stable views in a medium so perturbed and fleeting. This is no cabinet science, in which things are tested to a scruple; we theorise with a pistol to our head; we are confronted with a new set of conditions on which we have not only to pass a judgment, but to take action, before the hour is at an end. And we cannot even regard ourselves as a constant; in this flux of things, our identity itself seems in a perpetual variation; and not infrequently we find our own disguise the strangest in the masquerade. In the course of time, we grow to love things we hated and hate things we loved. Milton is not so dull as he once was, nor perhaps Ainsworth so amusing. It is decidedly harder to climb trees, and not nearly so hard to sit still. There is no use pretending; even the thrice royal game of hide and seek has somehow lost in zest. All our attributes are modified or changed; and it will be a poor account of us if our views do not modify and change in a proportion. To hold the same views at forty as we held at twenty is to have been stupefied for a score of years, and take rank, not as a prophet, but as an unteachable brat, well birched and none the wiser. It is as if a ship captain should sail to India from the Port of London; and having brought a chart of the Thames on deck at his first setting out, should obstinately use no other for the whole voyage.

And mark you, it would be no less foolish to begin at Gravesend with a chart of the Red Sea. *Si Jeunesse savait, si Vieillesse pouvait,* is a very pretty sentiment, but not necessarily right. In five cases out of ten, it is not so much that the young people do not know, as that they do not choose. There is something irreverent in the speculation, but perhaps the want of power has more to do with the wise resolutions of age than we are always willing to admit. It would be an instructive experiment to make an old man young again and leave him all his savoir. I scarcely think he would put his money in the Savings Bank after all; I doubt if he would be such an admirable son as we are led to expect; and as for his conduct in love, I believe firmly he would out-Herod Herod, and put the whole of his new compeers to the blush. Prudence is a wooden juggernaut, before whom Benjamin Franklin walks with the portly air of a high priest, and after whom dances many a successful merchant in the character of Atys. But it is not a deity to cultivate in youth. If a man lives to any considerable age, it cannot be denied that he laments his imprudences, but I notice he often laments his youth a deal more bitterly and with a more genuine intonation.

It is customary to say that age should be considered, because it comes last. It seems just as much to the point, that youth comes first. And the scale fairly kicks the beam, if you go on to add that age, in a majority of cases, never comes at all. Disease and accident make short work of even the most prosperous persons; death costs nothing, and the expense of a headstone is an inconsiderable trifle to the happy heir. To be suddenly snuffed out in the middle of ambitious schemes, is tragical enough at best; but when a man has been grudging himself

his own life in the meanwhile, and saving up everything for
the festival that was never to be, it becomes that hysterically
moving sort of tragedy which lies on the confines of farce. The
victim is dead—and he has cunningly overrreached himself: a
combination of calamities none the less absurd for being grim.
To husband a favourite claret until the batch turns sour, is not
at all an artful stroke of policy; and how much more with a
whole cellar—a whole bodily existence! People may lay down
their lives with cheerfulness in the sure expectation of a blessed
immortality; but that is a different affair from giving up youth
with all its admirable pleasures, in the hope of a better quality
of gruel in a more than problematical, nay, more than improb-
able, old age. We should not compliment a hungry man, who
should refuse a whole dinner and reserve all his appetite for the
dessert, before he knew whether there was to be any dessert or
not. If there be such a thing as imprudence in the world, we
surely have it here. We sail in leaky bottoms and on great and
perilous waters; and to take a cur from the dolorous old naval
ballad, we have heard the mermaidens singing, and know that
we shall never see dry land any more. Old and young, we are
all on our last cruise. If there is a fill of tobacco among the
crew, for God's sake pass it round, and let us have a pipe
before we go!

Indeed, by the report of our elders, this nervous preparation
for old age is only trouble thrown away. We fall on guard, and
after all it is a friend who comes to meet us. After the sun is
down and the west faded, the heavens begin to fill with shining
stars. So, as we grow old, a sort of equable jog-trot of feeling
is substituted for the violent ups and downs of passion and
disgust; the same influence that restrains our hopes, quiets our
apprehensions; if the pleasures are less intense, the troubles
are milder and more tolerable; and in a word, this period for
which we are asked to hoard up everything as for a time of

famine, is, in its own right, the richest, easiest, and happiest of life. Nay, by managing its own work and following its own happy inspiration, youth is doing the best it can to endow the leisure of age. A full, busy youth is your only prelude to a self-contained and independent age; and the muff inevitably develops into the bore. There are not many Doctor Johnsons, to set forth upon their first romantic voyage at sixty-four. If we wish to scale Mont Blanc or visit a thieves' kitchen in the East End, to go down in a diving dress or up in a balloon, we must be about it while we are still young. It will not do to delay until we are clogged with prudence and limping with rheumatism, and people begin to ask us: "What does Gravity out of bed?" Youth is the time to go flashing from one end of the world to the other both in mind and body; to try the manners of different nations; to hear the chimes at midnight; to see sunrise in town and country; to be converted at a revival; to circumnavigate the metaphysics, write halting verses, run a mile to see a fire, and wait all day long in the theatre to applaud Hernani. There is some meaning in the old theory about wild oats; and a man who has not had his green-sickness and got done with it for good, is as little to be depended on as an unvaccinated infant.

"It is extraordinary," says Lord Beaconsfield, one of the brightest and best preserved of youths up to the date of his last novel,[1] "it is extraordinary how hourly and how violently change the feelings of an inexperienced young man." And this mobility is a special talent entrusted to his care; a sort of indestructible virginity; a magic armour, with which he can pass unhurt through great dangers and come unbedaubed out of the miriest passages. Let him voyage, speculate, see all that he can, do all that he may; his soul has as many lives as a cat, he will live in all weathers, and never be a halfpenny the worse.

---

[1] *Lothair.*

Those who go to the devil in youth, with anything like a fair chance, were probably little worth saving from the first; they must have been feeble fellows—creatures made of putty and pack-thread, without steel or fire, anger or true joyfulness, in their composition; we may sympathise with their parents, but there is not much cause to go into mourning for themselves; for to be quite honest, the weak brother is the worst of mankind.

When the old man waggles his head and says, "Ah, so I thought when I was your age," he has proved the youth's case. Doubtless, whether from growth of experience or decline of animal heat, he thinks so no longer; but he thought so while he was young; and all men have thought so while they were young, since there was dew in the morning or hawthorn in May; and here is another young man adding his vote to those of previous generations and rivetting another link to the chain of testimony. It is as natural and as right for a young man to be imprudent and exaggerated, to live in swoops and circles, and beat about his cage like any other wild thing newly captured, as it is for old men to turn grey, or mothers to love their offspring, or heroes to die for something worthier than their lives.

By way of an apologue for the aged, when they feel more than usually tempted to offer their advice, let me recommend the following little tale. A child who had been remarkably fond of toys (and in particular of lead soldiers) found himself growing to the level of acknowledged boyhood without any abatement of this childish taste. He was thirteen; already he had been taunted for dallying overlong about the playbox; he had to blush if he was found among his lead soldiers; the shades of the prison-house were closing about him with a vengeance. There is nothing more difficult than to put the thoughts of children into the language of their elders; but this is the effect of his meditations at this juncture: "Plainly," he said, "I must give up my playthings, in the meanwhile, since I am not in a position to secure myself against idle jeers. At the same time, I am sure that playthings are the very pick of life; all people give them up out of the same pusillanimous respect for those who are a little older; and if they do not return to them as soon as they can, it is only because they grow stupid and forget. I shall be wiser; I shall conform for a little to the ways of their foolish world; but so soon as I have made enough money, I shall retire and shut myself up among my playthings until the day I die." Nay, as he was passing in the train along the Esterel mountains between Cannes and Fréjus, he remarked a pretty house in an orange garden at the angle of a bay, and decided that this should be his Happy Valley. *Astrea Redux; childhood* was to come again! The idea has an air of simple nobility to me, not unworthy of Cincinnatus. And yet, as the reader has probably anticipated, it is never likely to be carried into effect. There was a worm in the bud, a fatal error in the premises. Childhood must pass away, and then youth, as surely as age approaches. The true wisdom is to be always seasonable, and to change with a good grace in changing circumstances. To love playthings well as a child, to lead an adventurous and honourable youth, and to settle when the time arrives, into a green and smiling age, is to be a good artist in life and deserve well of yourself and your neighbour.

You need repent none of your youthful vagaries. They may have been over the score on one side, just as those of age are probably over the score on the other. But they had a point; they not only befitted your age and expressed its attitude and passions, but they had a relation to what was outside of you, and implied criticisms on the existing state of things, which you need not allow to have been undeserved because you now see that they were partial. All error, not merely verbal, is a strong way of stating that the current truth is incomplete. The follies of youth have a basis in sound reason, just as much as the embarrassing questions put by babes and sucklings. Their most antisocial acts indicate the defects of our society. When the torrent sweeps the man against a boulder, you must expect him to scream, and you need not be surprised if the scream is sometimes a theory. Shelley, chafing at the Church of England, discovered the cure of all evils in universal atheism. Generous lads irritated at the injustices of society, see nothing for it but the abolishment of everything and Kingdom Come of anarchy. Shelley was a young fool; so are these cocksparrow revolutionaries. But it is better to be a fool than to be dead. It is better to emit a scream in the shape of a theory than to be entirely insensible to the jars and incongruities of life and take everything as it comes in a forlorn stupidity. Some people swallow the universe like a pill; they travel on through the world like smiling images pushed from behind. For God's sake give me the young man who has brains enough to make a fool of himself! As for the others, the irony of facts shall take it out of their hands, and make fools of them in down-earnest, ere the farce be over. There shall be such a mopping and a mowing at the last day, and such blushing and confusion of countenance for all those who have been wise in their own esteem, and have not learnt the rough lessons that youth hands on to age. If we are indeed here to perfect and complete our own natures, and grow larger, stronger, and more sympathetic against some nobler career in the future, we had all best bestir ourselves to the utmost while we have the time. To equip a dull, respectable person with wings would be but to make a parody of an angel.

In short, if youth is not quite right in its opinions, there is a strong probability that age is not much more so. Undying hope is co-ruler of the human bosom with infallible credulity. A man finds he has been wrong at every preceding stage of his career, only to deduce the astonishing conclusion that he is at last entirely right. Mankind, after centuries of failure, are still upon the eve of a thoroughly constitutional millennium. Since we have explored the maze so long without result, it follows, for poor human reason, that we cannot have to explore much longer; close by must be the centre, with a champagne luncheon and a piece of ornamental water. How if there were no centre at all, but just one alley after another, and the whole world a labyrinth without end or issue?

I overheard the other day a scrap of conversation, which I take the liberty to reproduce. "What I advance is true," said one. "But not the whole truth," answered the other. "Sir," returned the first (and it seemed to me there was a smack of Dr. Johnson in the speech), "Sir, there is no such thing as the whole truth!" Indeed, there is nothing so evident in life as that there are two sides to a question. History is one long illustration. The forces of nature are engaged, day by day, in cudgelling it into our backward intelligences. We never pause for a moment's consideration, but we admit it as an axiom. An enthusiast sways humanity exactly by disregarding this great truth, and dinning it into our ears that this or that question has only one possible solution; and your enthusiast is a fine florid fellow, dominates things for a while and shakes the world out of a doze; but when once he is gone, an army of quiet and uninfluential people set to work to remind us of the other side and demolish the generous imposture. While Calvin is putting everybody exactly right in his Institutes, and hot-headed Knox is thundering in the pulpit, Montaigne is already looking at the other side in his library in Perigord, and predicting that they will find as much to quarrel about in the Bible as they had found already in the Church. Age may have one side, but assuredly Youth has the other. There is nothing more certain than that both are right, except perhaps that both are wrong. Let them agree to differ; for who knows but what agreeing to differ may not be a form of agreement rather than a form of difference?

I suppose it is written that any one who sets up for a bit of a philosopher, must contradict himself to his very face. For here have I fairly talked myself into thinking that we have the whole thing before us at last; that there is no answer to the mystery, except that there are as many as you please; that there is no centre to the maze because, like the famous sphere, its centre is everywhere; and that agreeing to differ with every ceremony of politeness, is the only "one undisturbed song of pure concent" to which we are ever likely to lend our musical voices.

I I

Child's Play

The regret we have for our childhood is not wholly justifiable: so much a man may lay down without fear of public ribaldry; for although we shake our heads over the change, we are not unconscious of the manifold advantages of our new state. What we lose in generous impulse, we more than gain in the habit of generously watching others; and the capacity to enjoy Shakespeare may balance a lost aptitude for playing at soldiers. Terror is gone out of our lives, moreover; we no longer see the devil in the bed-curtains nor lie awake to listen to the wind. We go to school no more; and if we have only exchanged one drudgery for another (which is by no means sure), we are set free for ever from the daily fear of chastisement. And yet a great change has overtaken us; and although we do not enjoy ourselves less, at least we take our pleasure differently. We need pickles nowadays to make Wednesday's cold mutton please our Friday's appetite; and I can remember the time when to call it red venison, and tell myself a hunter's story, would have made it more palatable than the best of sauces. To the grown person, cold mutton is cold mutton all the world over; not all the mythology ever invented by man will make it better or worse to him; the broad fact. the clamant reality, of the mutton carries away before it such seductive figments. But for the child it is still possible to weave an

33

enchantment over eatables; and if he has but read of a dish in a storybook, it will be heavenly manna to him for a week.

If a grown man does not like eating and drinking and exercise, if he is not something positive in his tastes, it means he has a feeble body and should have some medicine; but children may be pure spirits, if they will, and take their enjoyment in a world of moonshine. Sensation does not count for so much in our first years as afterwards; something of the swaddling numbness of infancy clings about us; we see and hear through a sort of golden mist. Children, for instance, are able enough to see, but they have no great faculty for looking; they do not use their eyes for the pleasure of using them, but for by-ends of their own; and the things I call to mind seeing most vividly, were not beautiful in themselves, but merely interesting or enviable to me as I thought they might be turned to practical account in play. Nor is the sense of touch so clean and poignant in children as it is in a man. If you will turn over your old memories, I think the sensations of this sort you remember will be somewhat vague, and come to not much more than a blunt, general sense of heat on summer days, or a blunt, general sense of wellbeing in bed. And here, of course, you will understand pleasurable sensations; for overmastering pain—the most deadly and tragical element in life, and the true commander of man's soul and body—alas! pain has its own way with all of us; it breaks in, a rude visitant, upon the fairy garden where the child wanders in a dream, no less surely than it rules upon the field of battle, or sends the immortal war-god whimpering to his father; and innocence, no more than philosophy, can protect us from this sting. As for taste, when we bear in mind the excesses of unmitigated sugar which delight a youthful palate, "it is surely no very cynical asperity" to think taste a character of the maturer growth. Smell and hearing are perhaps more developed; I remember many scents, many voices, and a great deal of spring singing in the woods. But hearing is capable of vast improvement as a means of pleasure; and there is all the world between gaping wonderment at the jargon of birds, and the emotion with which a man listens to articulate music.

At the same time, and step by step with this increase in the definition and intensity of what we feel which accompanies our growing age, another change takes place in the sphere of intellect, by which all things are transformed and seen through theories and associations as through coloured windows. We make to ourselves day by day, out of history, and gossip, and economical speculations, and God knows what, a medium in which we walk and through which we look abroad. We study shop windows with other eyes than in our childhood, never to wonder, not always to admire, but to make and modify our little incongruous theories about life. It is no longer the uniform of a soldier that arrests our attention; but perhaps the flowing carriage of a woman, or perhaps a countenance that has been vividly stamped with passion and carries an adventurous story written in its lines. The pleasure of surprise is passed away; sugar-loaves and water-carts seem mighty tame to encounter; and we walk the streets to make romances and to sociologise. Nor must we deny that a good many of us walk them solely for the purposes of transit or in the interest of a livelier digestion. These, indeed, may look back with mingled thoughts upon their childhood, but the rest are in a better case; they know more than when they were children, they understand better, their desires and sympathies answer more nimbly to the provocation of the senses, and their minds are brimming with interest as they go about the world.

According to my contention, this is a flight to which children cannot rise. They are wheeled in perambulators or dragged about by nurses in a pleasing stupor. A vague, faint, abiding wonderment possess them. Here and there some specially remarkable circumstances, such as a water-cart or a guardsman, fairly penetrates into the seat of thought and calls them, for half a moment, out of themselves; and you may see them, still towed forward sideways by the inexorable nurse as by a sort of destiny, but still staring at the bright object in their wake. It may be some minutes before another such moving spectacle reawakens them to the world in which they dwell. For other children, they almost invariably show some intelligent sympathy. "There is a fine fellow making mud pies," they seem to say: "that I can understand, there is some sense in mud pies." But the doings of their elders, unless where they are speakingly picturesque or recommend themselves by the quality of being easily imitable, they let them go over their heads (as we say) without the least regard. If it were not for this perpetual imitation, we should be tempted to fancy they despised us outright, or only considered us in the light of creatures brutally strong and brutally silly; among whom they condescended to dwell in obedience like a philosopher at a barbarous court. At times, indeed, they display an arrogance of disregard that is truly staggering. Once, when I was groaning aloud with physical pain, a young gentleman came into the room and nonchalantly inquired if I had seen his bow and arrow. He made no account of my groans, which he accepted, as he had to accept so much else, as a piece of the inexplicable conduct of his elders; and like a wise young gentleman, he would waste no wonder on the subject. Those elders, who care so little for rational enjoyment, and are even the enemies of rational enjoyment for others, he had accepted without understanding and without complaint, as the rest of us accept the scheme of the universe.

We grown people can tell ourselves a story, give and take strokes until the bucklers ring, ride far and fast, marry, fall, and die; all the while sitting quietly by the fire or lying prone in bed. This is exactly what a child cannot do, or does not do, at least, when he can find anything else. He works all with lay figures and stage properties. When his story comes to the fighting, he must rise, get something by way of a sword and have a set-to with a piece of furniture, until he is out of breath. When he comes to ride with the king's pardon, he must bestride a chair, which he will so hurry and belabour and on which he will so furiously demean himself, that the messenger will arrive, if not bloody with spurring, at least fiery red with haste. If his romance involves an accident upon a cliff, he must clamber in person about the chest of drawers and fall bodily upon the carpet, before his imagination is satisfied. Lead soldiers, dolls, all toys, in short, are in the same category and answer the same end. Nothing can stagger a child's faith; he accepts the clumsiest substitutes and can swallow the most staring incongruities. The chair he has just been besieging as a castle, or valiantly cutting to the ground as a dragon, is taken away for the accommodation of a morning visitor, and he is nothing abashed; he can skirmish by the hour with a stationary coal-scuttle; in the midst of the enchanted pleasance, he can see, without sensible shock, the gardener soberly digging potatoes for the day's dinner. He can make abstraction of whatever does not fit into his fable; and he puts his eyes into his pocket, just as we hold our noses in an unsavoury lane. And so it is, that although the ways of children cross with those of their elders in a hundred places daily, they never go in the same direction nor so much as lie in the same element. So may the telegraph wires intersect the line of the highroad, or so might a landscape painter and a bagman visit the same country, and yet move in different worlds.

People struck with these spectacles, cry aloud about the power of imagination in the young. Indeed there may be two words to that. It is, in some ways, but a pedestrian fancy that the child exhibits. It is the grown people who make the nursery stories; all the children do, is jealously to preserve the text. One out of a dozen reasons why Robinson Crusoe should be so popular with youth, is that it hits their level in this matter to a nicety; Crusoe was always at makeshifts and had, in so many words, to play at a great variety of professions; and then the book is all about tools, and there is nothing that delights a child so much. Hammers and saws belong to a province of life that positively calls for imitation. The juvenile lyrical drama, surely of the most ancient Thespian model, wherein the trades of mankind are successively simulated to the running burthen "On a cold and frosty morning," gives a good instance of the artistic taste in children. And this need for overt action and lay figures testifies to a defect in the child's imagination which prevents him from carrying out his novels in the privacy of his own heart. He does not yet know enough of the world and men. His experience is incomplete. That stage-wardrobe and scene-room that we call the memory is so ill provided, that he can overtake few combinations and body out few stories, to his own content, without some external aid. He is at the experimental stage; he is not sure how one would feel in certain circumstances; to make sure, he must come as near trying it as his means permit. And so here is young heroism with a wooden sword, and mothers practise their kind vocation over a bit of jointed stick. It may be laughable enough just now; but it is these same people and these same thoughts, that not long hence, when they are on the theatre of life, will make you weep and tremble. For children think very much the same thoughts and dream the same dreams, as bearded men and marriageable women. No one is more romantic. Fame and honour, the love of young men and the love of mothers, the business man's pleasure in method, all these and others they anticipate and rehearse in their play hours. Upon us, who are further advanced and fairly dealing with the threads of destiny, they only glance from time to time to glean a hint for their own mimetic reproduction. Two children playing at soldiers are far more interesting to each other than one of the scarlet beings whom both are busy imitating. This is perhaps the greatest oddity of all. "Art for Art" is their motto; and the doings of grown folk are only interesting as the raw material for play. Not Théophile Gautier, not Flaubert, can look more callously upon life, or rate the reproduction more highly over the reality; and they will parody an execution, a deathbed or the funeral of the young man of Nain, with all the cheerfulness in the world.

The true parallel for play is not to be found, of course, in conscious art, which, though it be derived from play, is itself an abstract, impersonal thing, and depends largely upon philosophical interests beyond the scope of childhood. It is when we make castles in the air and personate the leading character in our own romances, that we return to the spirit of our first years. Only, there are several reasons why the spirit is no longer so agreeable to indulge. Nowadays, when we admit this personal element in to our divagations we are apt to stir up uncomfortable and sorrowful memories, and remind ourselves sharply of old wounds. Our day-dreams can no longer lie all in the air like a story in the Arabian Nights; they read to us rather like the history of a period in which we ourselves had taken part, where we come across many unfortunate passages and find our own conduct smartly reprimanded. And then the child, mind you, acts his parts. He does not merely repeat them to himself; he leaps, he runs, and sets the blood agog over all his body. And so his play breathes him; and he no sooner assumes a passion than he gives it vent. Alas! when we betake ourselves to our intellectual form of play, sitting quietly by the fire or lying prone in bed, we rouse many hot feelings for which we can find no outlet. Substitutes are not acceptable to the mature mind, which desires the thing itself; and even to rehearse a triumphant dialogue with one's enemy, although it is perhaps the most satisfactory piece of play still left within our reach, is not entirely satisfying, and is even apt to lead to a visit and an interview which may be the reverse of triumphant after all.

In the child's world of dim sensation, play is all in all. "Making believe" is the gist of his whole life, and he cannot so much as take a walk except in character. I could not learn my alphabet without some suitable *mise-en-scène,* and had to act a business man in an office before I could sit down to my book. Will you kindly question your memory, and find out how much you did, work or pleasure, in good faith and soberness, and for how much you had to cheat yourself with some invention? I remember, as though it were yesterday, the expansion of spirit, the dignity and self-reliance, that came with a pair of mustachios in burnt cork, even when there was none to see. Children are even content to forego what we call the realities and prefer the shadow to the substance. When they might be speaking intelligibly together, they chatter senseless gibberish by the hour, and are quite happy because they are making believe to speak French. I have said already how even the imperious appetite of hunger suffers itself to be gulled and led by the nose with the fag end of an old song. And it goes deeper than this: when children are together even a meal is felt as an interruption in the business of life; and they must find some imaginative sanction, and tell themselves some sort of story, to account for, to colour, to render entertaining, the simple processes of eating and drinking. What wonderful fancies I have heard evolved out of the pattern upon tea-cups!—from which there followed a code of rules and a whole world of excitement, until tea-drinking began to take rank as a game. When my cousin and I took our porridge of a morning, we had a device to enliven the course of the meal. He ate his with sugar, and explained it to be a country continually buried under snow. I took mine with milk, and explained it to be a country suffering gradual inundation. You can imagine us exchanging bulletins; how here was an island still unsubmerged, here a valley not yet covered with snow; what inventions were made; how his population lived in cabins on perches and travelled on stilts, and how mine was always in boats; how the interest grew furious, as the last corner of safe ground was cut off on all sides and grew smaller every moment; and how, in fine, the food was of altogether secondary importance, and might even have been nauseous, so long as we seasoned it with these dreams. But perhaps the most exciting moments I ever had over a meal, were in the case of calves' feet jelly. It was hardly possible not to believe—and you may be sure, so far from trying, I did all I could to favour the illusion—that some part of it was hollow, and that sooner or later my spoon would lay open the secret tabernacle of the golden rock. There, might some miniature *Red Beard* await his hour; there, might one find the treasures of the *Forty Thieves,* and bewildered Cassim beating about the walls. And so I quarried on slowly, with bated breath, savouring the interest. Believe me, I had little palate left for the jelly; and though I preferred the taste when I took cream with it, I used often to go without, because the cream dimmed the transparent fractures.

Even with games, this spirit is authoritative with right-minded children. It is thus that hide-and-seek has so pre-eminent a sovereignty, for it is the well-spring of romance, and the actions and the excitement to which it gives rise lend themselves to almost any sort of fable. And thus cricket, which is a mere matter of dexterity, palpably about nothing and for no end, often fails to satisfy infantile craving. It is a game, if you like, but not a game of play. You cannot tell yourself a story about cricket; and the activity it calls forth can be justified on no rational theory. Even football, although it admirably simulates the tug and the ebb and flow of battle, has presented difficulties to the mind of young sticklers after verisimilitude; and I knew at least one little boy who was mightily exercised about the presence of the ball, and had to spirit himself up, whenever he came to play, with an elaborate story of enchantment, and take the missile as a sort of talisman bandied about in conflict between two Arabian nations.

To think of such a frame of mind, is to become disquieted about the bringing up of children. Surely they dwell in a mythological epoch, and are not the contemporaries of their parents. What can they think of them? what can they make of these bearded or petticoated giants who look down upon their games? who move upon a cloudy Olympus, following unknown designs apart from rational enjoyment? who profess the tenderest solicitude for children, and yet every now and again reach down out of their altitude and terribly vindicate the prerogatives of age? Off goes the child, corporally smarting, but morally rebellious. Were there ever such unthinkable deities as parents? I would give a great deal to know what, in nine cases out of ten, is the child's unvarnished feeling. A sense of past cajolery; a sense of personal attraction, at best very feeble; above all, I should imagine, a sense of terror for the untried residue of mankind: go to make up the attraction, that he feels. No wonder, poor little heart, with such a weltering world in front of him, if he clings to the hand he knows! The dread irrationality of the whole affair, as it seems to children, is a thing we are all too ready to forget. "O, why," I remember passionately wondering, "why can we not all be happy and devote ourselves to play?" And when children do philosophise, I believe it is usually to very much the same purpose.

One thing, at least, comes very clearly out of these considerations; that whatever we are to expect at the hands of children, it should not be any peddling exactitude about matters of fact. They walk in a vain show, and among mists and rainbows; they are passionate after dreams and unconcerned about realities; speech is a difficult art not wholly learned; and there is nothing in their own tastes or purposes to teach them what we mean by abstract truthfulness. When a bad writer is inexact, even if he can look back on half a century of years, we charge him with incompetence and not with dishonesty. And why not extend the same allowance to imperfect speakers? Let a stockbroker be dead stupid about poetry, or a poet inexact in the details of business, and we excuse them heartily from blame. But show us a miserable, unbreeched, human entity, whose whole profession it is to take a tub for a fortified town and a shaving-brush for the deadly stiletto, and who passes three-fourths of his time in a dream and the rest in open self-deception, and we expect him to be as nice upon a matter of fact as a scientific expert bearing evidence. Upon my heart, I think it less than decent. You do not consider how little the child sees, or how swift he is to weave what he has seen into bewildering fiction; and that he cares no more for what you call truth, than you for a gingerbread dragoon.

I am reminded, as I write, that the child is very inquiring as to the precise truth of stories. But indeed this is a very different matter, and one bound up with the subject of play, and the precise amount of playfulness, or playability, to be looked for in the world. Many such burning questions must arise in the course of nursery education. Among the fauna of this planet, which already embraces the pretty soldier and the terrifying Irish beggarman, is, or is not, the child to expect a Bluebeard or a Cormoran? Is he, or is he not, to look out for magicians, kindly and potent? May he, or may he not, reasonably hope to be cast away upon a desert island, or turned to such diminutive proportions that he can live on equal terms with his lead soldiery, and go a cruise in his own toy schooner? Surely all these are practical questions to a neophyte entering upon life with a view to play. Precision upon such a point, the child can understand. But if you merely ask him of his past behaviour, as to who threw such a stone, for instance, or struck such and such a match; or whether he had looked into a parcel or gone by a forbidden path—why, he can see no moment in the inquiry, and it is ten to one, he has already half forgotten and half bemused himself with subsequent imaginings.

It would be easy to leave them in their native cloud-land, where they figure so prettily—pretty like flowers and innocent like dogs. They will come out of their gardens soon enough, and have to go into offices and the witness-box. Spare them yet awhile, O conscientious parent! Let them doze among their playthings yet a little! for who knows what a rough, warfaring existence lies before them in the future?

III

Aes Triplex

The changes wrought by death are in themselves so sharp and final, and so terrible and melancholy in their consequences, that the thing stands alone in man's experience, and has no parallel upon earth. It outdoes all other accidents because it is the last of them. Sometimes it leaps suddenly upon its victims, like a Thug; sometimes it lays a regular siege and creeps upon their citadel during a score of years. And when the business is done, there is sore havoc made in other people's lives, and a pin knocked out by which many subsidiary friendships hung together. There are empty chairs, solitary walks, and single beds at night. Again, in taking away our friends, death does not take them away utterly, but leaves behind a mocking, tragical, and soon intolerable residue, which must be hurriedly concealed. Hence a whole chapter of sights and customs striking to the mind, from the pyramids of Egypt to the gibbets and dule trees of mediæval Europe. The poorest persons have a bit of pageant going towards the tomb; memorial stones are set up over the least memorable; and, in order to preserve some show of respect for what remains of our old loves and friendships, we must accompany it with much grimly ludicrous ceremonial, and the hired undertaker parades before the door. All this, and much more of the same sort, accompanied by the eloquence of poets, has gone a great way to put humanity in error; nay, in many philosophies the error has been embodied and laid down with every circumstance of logic; although in real life the bustle and swiftness, in leaving people little time to think, have not left them time enough to go dangerously wrong in practice.

As a matter of fact, although few things are spoken of with more fearful whisperings than this prospect of death, few have less influence on conduct under healthy circumstances. We have all heard of cities in South America built upon the side of fiery mountains, and how, even in this tremendous neighbourhood, the inhabitants are not a jot more impressed by the solemnity of mortal conditions than if they were delving gardens in the greenest corner of England. There are serenades and suppers and much gallantry among the myrtles overhead; and meanwhile the foundation shudders underfoot, the bowels of the mountain growl, and at any moment living ruin may leap sky-high into the moonlight, and tumble man and his merry-making in the dust. In the eyes of very young people, and very dull old ones, there is something indescribably reckless and desperate in such a picture. It seems not credible that respectable married people, with umbrellas, should find appetite for a bit of supper within quite a long distance of a fiery mountain; ordinary life begins to smell of high-handed debauch when it is carried on so close to a catastrophe; and even cheese and salad, it seems, could hardly be relished in such circumstances without something like a defiance of the Creator. It should be a place for nobody but hermits dwelling in prayer and maceration, or mere born-devils drowning care in a perpetual carouse.

And yet, when one comes to think upon it calmly, the situation of these South American citizens forms only a very pale figure for the state of ordinary mankind. This world itself, travelling blindly and swiftly in overcrowded space, among a million other worlds travelling blindly and swiftly in contrary directions, may very well come by a knock that would set it into explosion like a penny squib. And what, pathologically looked at, is the human body with all its organs, but a mere bagful of petards? The least of these is as dangerous to the whole economy as the ship's powder-magazine to the ship; and with every breath we breathe, and every meal we eat, we are putting one or more of them in peril. If we clung as devotedly as some philosophers pretend we do to the abstract idea of life, or were half as frightened as they make out we are, for the subversive accident that ends it all, the trumpets might sound by the hour and no one would follow them into battle— the blue-peter might fly at the truck, but who would climb into a sea-going ship? Think (if these philosophers were right) with what a preparation of spirit we should affront the daily peril of the dinner-table: a deadlier spot than any battle-field in history, where the far greater proportion of our ancestors have miserably left their bones! What woman would ever be lured into marriage, so much more dangerous than the wildest sea? And what would it be to grow old? For, after a certain distance, every step we take in life we find the ice growing thinner below our feet, and all around us and behind us we see our contemporaries going through. By the time a man gets well into the seventies, his continued existence is a mere miracle; and when he lays his old bones in bed for the night, there is an overwhelming probability that he will never see the day. Do the old men mind it, as a matter of fact? Why, no. They were never merrier; they have their grog at night, and tell the raciest stories; they hear of the death of people about their own age, or even younger, not as if it was a grisly warning, but with a simple child-like pleasure at having outlived some one else; and when a draught might puff them out like a gutter- ing candle, or a bit of a stumble shatter them like so much glass, their old hearts keep sound and unaffrighted, and they go on, bubbling with laughter, through years of man's age compared to which the valley at Balaclava was as safe and peaceful as a village cricket-green on Sunday. It may fairly be questioned (if we look to the peril only) whether it was a much more daring feat for Curtius to plunge into the gulf, than for any old gentleman of ninety to doff his clothes and clamber into bed.

Indeed, it is a memorable subject for consideration, with what unconcern and gaiety mankind pricks on along the Valley of the Shadow of Death. The whole way is one wilderness of snares, and at the end of it, for those who fear the last pinch, is irrevocable ruin. And yet we go spinning through it all, like a party for the Derby. Perhaps the reader remembers one of the humourous devices of the deified Caligula: how he encouraged a vast concourse of holiday-makers on to his bridge over Baiae bay; and when they were in the height of their enjoyment, turned loose the Prætorian guards among the company, and had them tossed into the sea. This is no bad miniature of the dealings of nature with the transitory race of man. Only, what a chequered picnic we have of it, even while it lasts! and into what great waters, not to be crossed by any swimmer, God's pale Prætorian throws us over in the end!

We live the time that a match flickers; we pop the cork of a ginger-beer bottle, and the earthquake swallows us on the instant. Is it not odd, is it not incongruous, is it not, in the highest sense of human speech, incredible, that we should think so highly of the ginger-beer, and regard so little the devouring earthquake? The love of Life and the fear of Death are two famous phrases that grow harder to understand the more we think about them. It is a well-known fact that an immense proportion of boat accidents would never happen if people held the sheet in their hands instead of making it fast; and yet, unless it be some martinet of a professional mariner or some landsman with shattered nerve, every one of God's creatures makes it fast. A strange instance of man's unconcern and brazen boldness in the face of death!

We confound ourselves with metaphysical phrases, which we import into daily talk with noble inappropriateness. We have no idea of what death is, apart from its circumstances and some of its consequences to others; and although we have some experience of living, there is not a man on earth who has flown so high into abstraction as to have any practical guess at the meaning of the word life. All literature, from Job and Omar Khayyam to Thomas Çarlyle or Walt Whitman, is but an attempt to look upon the human state with such largeness of view as shall enable us to rise from the consideration of living to the Definition of Life. And our sages give us about the best satisfaction in their power when they say that it is a vapour, or a show, or made out of the same stuff with dreams. Philosophy, in its more rigid sense, has been at the same work for ages; and after a myriad bald heads have wagged over the problem, and piles of words have been heaped one upon another into dry and cloudy volumes without end, philosophy has the honour of laying before us, with modest pride, her contribution towards the subject: that life is a Permanent Possibility of Sensation. Truly a fine result! A man may very well love beef, or hunting, or a woman; but surely, surely, not a Permanent Possibility of Sensation! He may be afraid of a precipice, or a dentist, or a large enemy with a club, or even an undertaker's man; but not certainly of abstract death. We may trick with the word life in its dozen senses until we are weary of tricking; we may argue in terms of all the philosophies on earth, but one fact remains true throughout—that we do not love life, in the sense that we are greatly preoccupied about its conservation; that we do not, properly speaking, love life at all, but living. Into the views of the least careful there will enter some degree of providence; no man's eyes are fixed entirely on the passing hour; but although we have some anticipation of good health, good weather, wine, active employment, love, and self-approval, the sum of these anticipations does not amount to anything like a general view of life's possibilities and issues; nor are those who cherish them most vividly, at all the most scrupulous of their personal safety. To be deeply interested in the accidents of our existence, to enjoy keenly the mixed texture of human experience, rather leads a man to disregard precautions, and risk his neck against a straw. For surely the love of living is stronger in an Alpine climber roping over a peril, or a hunter riding merrily at a stiff fence, than in a creature who lives upon a diet and walks a measured distance in the interest of his constitution.

There is a great deal of very vile nonsense talked upon both sides of the matter: tearing divines reducing life to the dimensions of a mere funeral procession, so short as to be hardly decent; and melancholy unbelievers yearning for the tomb as if it were a world too far away. Both sides must feel a little ashamed of their performances now and again when they draw in their chairs to dinner. Indeed, a good meal and a bottle of wine is an answer to most standard works upon the question. When a man's heart warms to his viands, he forgets a great deal of sophistry, and soars into a rosy zone of contemplation. Death may be knocking at the door, like the Commander's statue; we have something else in hand, thank God, and let him knock. Passing bells are ringing all the world over. All the world over, and every hour, some one is parting company with all his aches and ecstasies. For us also the trap is laid. But we are so fond of life that we have no leisure to entertain the terror of death. It is a honeymoon with us all through, and one of the longest. Small blame to us if we give our whole hearts to this glowing bride of ours, to the appetites, to honour, to the hungry curiosity of the mind, to the pleasure of the eyes in nature, and the pride of our own nimble bodies.

We all of us appreciate the sensations; but as for caring about the Permanence of the Possibility, a man's head is generally very bald, and his senses very dull, before he comes to that. Whether we regard life as a lane leading to a dead wall—a mere bag's end, as the French say—or whether we think of it as a vestibule or gymnasium, where we wait our turn and prepare our faculties for some more noble destiny; whether we thunder in a pulpit, or pule in little atheistic poetry-books, about its vanity and brevity; whether we look justly for years of health and vigour, or are about to mount into a Bath-chair, as a step towards the hearse; in each and all of these views and situations there is but one conclusion possible: that a man should stop his ears against paralysing terror, and run the race that is set before him with a single mind. No one surely could have recoiled with more heartache and terror from the thought of death than our respected lexicographer; and yet we know how little it affected his conduct, how wisely and boldly he walked, and in what a fresh and lively vein he spoke of life. Already an old man, he ventured on his Highland tour; and his heart, bound with triple brass, did not recoil before twenty-seven individual cups of tea. As courage and intelligence are the two qualities best worth a good man's cultivation, so it is the first part of intelligence to recognise our precarious estate in life, and the first part of courage to be not at all abashed before the fact. A frank and somewhat headlong carriage, not looking too anxiously before, not dallying in maudlin regret over the past, stamps the man who is well armoured for this world.

And not only well armoured for himself, but a good friend and a good citizen to boot. We do not go to cowards for tender dealing; there is nothing so cruel as panic; the man who has least fear for his own carcass, has most time to consider others. That eminent chemist who took his walks abroad in tin shoes, and subsisted wholly upon tepid milk, had all his work cut out for him in considerate dealings with his own digestion. So soon as prudence has begun to grow up in the brain, like a dismal fungus, it finds its first expression in a paralysis of generous acts. The victim begins to shrink spiritually; he develops a fancy for parlours with a regulated temperature, and takes his morality on the principle of tin shoes and tepid milk. The care of one important body or soul becomes so engrossing, that all the noises of the outer world begin to come thin and faint into the parlour with the regulated temperature; and the tin shoes go equably forward over blood and rain. To be over-wise is to ossify; and the scruple-monger ends by standing stockstill. Now the man who has his heart on his sleeve, and a good whirling weathercock of a brain, who reckons his life as a thing to be dashingly used and cheerfully hazarded, makes a very different acquaintance of the world, keeps all his pulses going true and fast, and gathers impetus as he runs, until, if he be running towards anything better than wildfire, he may shoot up and become a constellation in the end. Lord look after his health, Lord have a care of his soul, says he; and he has at the key of the position, and swashes through incongruity and peril towards his aim. Death is on all sides of him with pointed batteries, as he is on all sides of all of us; unfortunate surprises gird him round; mim-mouthed* friends and relations hold up their hands in quite a little elegiacal synod about his path : and what cares he for all this? Being a true lover of living, a fellow with something pushing and spontaneous in his inside, he must, like any other soldier, in any other stirring, deadly warfare, push on at his best pace until he touch the goal. "A peerage or

* Primly reticent—Ed.

Westminster Abbey!" cried Nelson in his bright, boyish, heroic manner. These are great incentives; not for any of these, but for the plain satisfaction of living, of being about their business in some sort or other, do the brave, serviceable men of every nation tread down the nettle danger, and pass flyingly over all the stumbling-blocks of prudence. Think of the heroism of Johnson, think of that superb indifference to mortal limitation that set him upon his dictionary, and carried him through triumphantly until the end! Who, if he were wisely considerate of things at large, would ever embark upon any work much more considerable than a halfpenny post card? Who would project a serial novel, after Thackeray and Dickens had each fallen in mid-course? Who would find heart enough to begin to live, if he dallied with the consideration of death?

And, after all, what sorry and pitiful quibbling all this is! To forego all the issues of living in a parlour with a regulated temperature—as if that were not to die a hundred times over, and for ten years at a stretch! And if it were not to die in one's own lifetime, and without even the sad immunities of death! As if it were not to die, and yet be the patient spectators of our own pitiable change! The Permanent Possibility is preserved, but the sensations carefully held at arm's length, as if one kept a photographic plate in a dark chamber. It is better to lose health like a spendthrift than to waste it like a miser. It is better to live and be done with it, than to die daily in the sickroom. By all means begin your folio; even if the doctor does not give you a year, even if he hesitates about a month, make one brave push and see what can be accomplished in a week. It is not only in finished undertakings that we ought to honour useful labour. A spirit goes out of the man who means execution, which outlives the most untimely ending. All who have meant good work with their whole hearts, have done good work, although they may die before they have the time to sign it. Every heart that has beat strong and cheerfully has left a hopeful impulse behind it in the world, and bettered the tradition of mankind. And even if death catch people, like an open pitfall, and in mid-career, laying out vast projects, and planning monstrous foundations, flushed with hope, and their mouths full of boastful language, they should be at once tripped up and silenced: is there not something brave and spirited in such a termination? and does not life go down with a better grace, foaming in full body over a precipice, than miserably straggling to an end in sandy deltas? When the Greeks made their fine saying that those whom the gods love die young, I cannot help believing they had this sort of death also in their eye. For surely, at whatever age it overtake the man, this is to die young. Death has not been suffered to take so much as an allusion from his heart. In the hot-fit of life, a tip-toe on the highest point of being, he passes at a bound on to the other side. The noise of the mallet and chisel is scarcely quenched, the trumpets are hardly done blowing, when, trailing with him clouds of glory, this happy-starred, full-blooded spirit shoots into the spiritual land.

I V

Father Damien

An Open Letter to the Reverend Dr. Hyde of Honolulu

Sydney, February 25, 1890.

Sir—

It may probably occur to you that we have met, and visited, and conversed; on my side, with interest. You may remember that you have done me several courtesies, for which I was prepared to be grateful. But there are duties which come before gratitude, and offences which justly divide friends, far more acquaintances. Your letter to the Reverend H. B. Gage is a document, which, in my sight, if you had filled me with bread when I was starving, if you had sat up to nurse my father when he lay a-dying, would yet absolve me from the bonds of gratitude. You know enough, doubtless, of the process of canonisation to be aware that, a hundred years after the death of Damien, there will appear a man charged with the painful office of the devil's advocate. After that noble brother of mine, and of all frail clay, shall have lain a century at rest, one shall accuse, one defend him. The circumstance is unusual that the *devil's advocate* should be a volunteer, should be a member of a sect immediately rival, and should make haste to take upon himself his ugly office ere the bones are cold; unusual, and to me inspiring. If I have at all learned the trade of using words to convey truth and to arouse emotion, you have at last furnished

55

me with a subject. For it is in the interest of all mankind and the cause of public decency in every quarter of the world, not only that Damien should be righted, but that you and your letter should be displayed at length, in their true colours, to the public eye.

To do this properly, I must begin by quoting you at large: I shall then proceed to criticise your utterance from several points of view, divine and human, in the course of which I shall attempt to draw again and with more specification the character of the dead saint whom it has pleased you to vilify: so much being done, I shall say farewell to you for ever.

Honolulu, August 2, 1889.

"Rev. H. B. Gage.

"Dear Brother—

In answer to your inquiries about Father Damien, I can only reply that we who knew the man are surprised at the extravagant newspaper laudations, as if he was a most saintly philanthropist. The simple truth is, he was a coarse, dirty man, headstrong and bigoted. He was not sent to Molokai, but went there without orders; did not stay at the leper settlement (before he became one himself), but circulated freely over the whole island (less than half the island is devoted to the lepers), and he came often to Honolulu. He had no hand in the reforms and improvements inaugurated, which were the work of our Board of Health, as occasion required and means were provided. He was not a pure man in his relations with women, and the leprosy of which he died should be attributed to his vices and carelessness. Others have done much for the lepers, our own ministers, the government physicians, and so forth, but never with the Catholic idea of meriting eternal life.

Yours, etc.,

C. M. Hyde." [1]

[1] From the Sydney Presbyterian, October 26, 1889.

To deal fitly with a letter so extraordinary, I must draw at the outset on my private knowledge of the signatory and his sect. It may offend others; scarcely you, who have been so busy to collect, so bold to publish, gossip on your rivals. And this is perhaps the moment when I may best explain to you the character of what you are to read: I conceive you as a man quite beyond·and below the reticences of civility: with what measure you mete, with that shall it be measured you again; with you, at last, I rejoice to feel the button off the foil and to plunge home. And if in aught that I shall say I should offend others, your colleagues, whom I respect and remember with affection, I can but offer them my regret; I am not free, I am inspired by the consideration of interests far more large; and such pain as can be inflicted by anything from me must be indeed trifling when compared with the pain with which they read your letter. It is not the hangman, but the criminal, that brings dishonour on the house.

You belong, sir, to a sect—I believe my sect, and that in which my ancestors laboured—which has enjoyed and partly failed to utilise, an exceptional advantage in the islands of Hawaii. The first missionaries came; they found the land already self-purged of its old and bloody faith; they were embraced, almost on their arrival, with enthusiasm; what troubles they supported came far more from whites than from Hawaiians; and to these last they stood (in a rough figure) in the shoes of God. This is not the place to enter into the degree or causes of their failure, such as it is. One element alone is pertinent, and must here be plainly dealt with. In the course of their evangelical calling, they—or too many of them—grew rich. It may be news to you that the houses of missionaries are a cause of mocking on the streets of Honolulu. It will at least be news to you, that when I returned your civil visit, the driver of my cab commented on the size, the taste, and the comfort of your home. It would have been news certainly to myself, had any one told me that afternoon that I should live to drag such matter into print. But you see, sir, how you degrade better men to your own level; and it is needful that those who are to judge betwixt you and me, betwixt Damien and the devil's advocate, should understand your letter to have been penned in a house which could raise, and that very justly, the envy and the comments of the passers-by. I think (to employ a phrase of yours which I admire) it "should be attributed" to you that you have never visited the scene of Damien's life and death. If you had, and had recalled it, and looked about your pleasant rooms, even your pen perhaps would have been stayed.

Your sect (and remember, as far as any sect avows me, it is mine) has not done ill in a worldly sense in the Hawaiian Kingdom. When calamity befell their innocent parishioners, when leprosy descended and took root in the Eight Islands, a *quid pro quo* was to be looked for. To that prosperous mission, and to you, as one of its adornments, God had sent at last an opportunity. I know I am touching here upon a nerve acutely sensitive. I know that others of your colleagues look back on the inertia of your Church, and the intrusive and decisive heroism of Damien, with something almost to be called remorse. I am sure it is so with yourself; I am persuaded your letter was inspired by a certain envy, not essentially ignoble, and the one human trait to be espied in that performance. You were thinking of the lost chance, the past day; of that which should have been conceived and was not; of the service due and not rendered. Time was, said the voice in your ear, in your pleasant room, as you sat raging and writing; and if the words written were base beyond parallel, the rage, I am happy to repeat—it is the only compliment I shall pay you—the rage was almost virtuous. But, sir, when we have failed, and another has succeeded; when we have stood by, and another has stepped in;

when we sit and grow bulky in our charming mansions, and a plain, uncouth peasant steps into the battle, under the eyes of God, and succours the afflicted, and consoles the dying, and is himself afflicted in his turn, and dies upon the field of honour —the battle cannot be retrieved as your unhappy irritation has suggested. It is a lost battle, and lost for ever. One thing remained to you in your defeat—some rags of common honour; and these you have made haste to cast away.

Common honour; not the honour of having done anything right, but the honour of not having done aught conspicuously foul; the honour of the inert: that was what remained to you. We are not all expected to be Damiens; a man may conceive his duty more narrowly, he may love his comforts better; and none will cast a stone at him for that. But will a gentleman of your reverend profession allow me an example from the fields of gallantry? When two gentlemen compete for the favour of a lady, and the one succeeds and the other is rejected, and (as will sometimes happen) matter damaging to the successful rival's credit reaches the ear of the defeated, it is held by plain men of no pretensions that his mouth is, in the circumstances, almost necessarily closed. Your Church and Damien's were in Hawaii upon a rivalry to do well: to help, to edify, to set divine examples. You have (in one huge instance) failed, and Damien succeeded, I marvel it should not have occurred to you that you were doomed to silence; that when you had been out-stripped in that high rivalry, and sat inglorious in the midst of your well-being, in your pleasant room—and Damien, crowned with glories and horrors, toiled and rotted in that pigstye of his under the cliffs of Kalawao—you, the elect who would not, were the last man on earth to collect and propagate gossip on the volunteer who would and did.

I think I see you—for I try to see you in the flesh as I write these sentences—I think I see you leap at the word pigstye, a hyperbolical expression at the best. "He had no hand in the reforms," he was "a coarse, dirty man"; these were your own words; and you may think it possible that I am come to support you with fresh evidence. In a sense, it is even so. Damien has been too much depicted with a conventional halo and conventional features; so drawn by men who perhaps had not the eye to remark or the pen to express the individual; or who perhaps were only blinded and silenced by generous admiration, such as I partly envy for myself—such as you, if your soul were enlightened, would envy on your bended knees. It is the least defect of such a method of portraiture that it makes the path easy for the devil's advocate, and leaves for the misuse of the slanderer a considerable field of truth. For the truth that is suppressed by friends is the readiest weapon of the enemy. The world, in your despite, may perhaps owe you something, if your letter be the means of substituting once for all a credible likeness for a wax abstraction. For, if that world at all remember you, on the day when Damien of Molokai shall be named Saint, it will be in virtue of one work: your letter to the Reverend H. B. Gage.

You may ask on what authority I speak. It was my inclement destiny to become acquainted, not with Damien, but with Dr. Hyde. When I visited the lazaretto Damien was already in his resting grave. But such information as I have, I gathered on the spot in conversation with those who knew him well and long: some indeed who revered his memory; but others who had sparred and wrangled with him, who beheld him with no halo, who perhaps regarded him with small respect, and through whose unprepared and scarcely partial communications the plain, human features of the man shone on me convincingly. These gave me what knowledge I possess; and I learnt it in that scene where it could be most completely and sensitively understood—Kalawao, which you have never visited, about which you have never so much as endeavoured to inform yourself: for, brief as your letter is, you have found the means to stumble into that confession. *"Less than one-half of the island,"* you say, "is devoted to the lepers." Molokai—*"Molokai ahima,"* the "grey," lofty, and most desolate island—along all its northern side plunges in front of precipice into a sea of unusual profundity. This range of cliff is, from east to west, the true end and frontier of the island. Only in one spot there projects into the ocean a certain triangular and rugged down, grassy, stony, windy, and rising in the midst into a hill with a dead crater: the whole bearing to the cliff that overhangs it somewhat the same relation as a bracket to a wall. With this hint you will now be able to pick out the leper station on a map; you will be able to judge how much of Molokai is thus cut off between the surf and precipice, whether less than a half, or less than a quarter, or a fifth, or a tenth—or say, a twentieth; and the next time you burst into print you will be in a position to share with us the issue of your calculations.

I imagine you to be one of those persons who talk with cheerfulness of that place which oxen and wainropes could not drag you to behold. You, who do not even know its situation on the map, probably denounce sensational descriptions, stretching your limbs the while in your pleasant parlour on Beretania Street. When I was pulled ashore there one early morning, there sat with me in the boat two sisters, bidding farewell (in humble imitation of Damien) to the lights and joys of human life. One of these wept silently; I could not withhold myself from joining her. Had you been there, it is my belief that nature would have triumphed even in you; and as the boat drew but a little nearer, and you beheld the stairs crowded with abominable deformations of our common manhood, and saw yourself landing in the midst of such a population as only now and then surrounds us in the horror of a nightmare—what a haggard eye you would have rolled over your reluctant shoulder towards the house on Beretania Street! Had you gone on; had you found every fourth face a blot upon the landscape; had you visited the hospital and seen the butt-ends of human beings lying there almost unrecognisable, but still breathing, still thinking, still remembering; you would have understood that life in the lazaretto is an ordeal from which the nerves of a man's spirit shrink, even as his eye quails under the brightness of the sun; you would have felt it was (even to-day) a pitiful place to visit and a hell to dwell in. It is not the fear of possible infection. That seems a little thing when compared with the pain, the pity, and the disgust of the visitor's surroundings, and the atmosphere of affliction, disease, and physical disgrace in which he breathes. I do not think I am a man more than usually timid; but I never recall the days and nights I spent upon that island promontory (eight days and seven nights), without heartfelt thankfulness that I am somewhere else. I find in my diary that I speak of my stay as a "grinding experience": I have once jotted in the margin, "Harrowing is the word"; and when the Mokoli bore me at last towards the outer world, I kept repeating to myself, with a new conception of their pregnancy, those simple words of the song—

> " 'Tis the most distressful country that ever
> yet was seen."

And observe: that which I saw and suffered from was a settlement purged, bettered, beautified; the new village built, the hospital and the Bishop-Home excellently arranged; the sisters, the doctor, and the missionaries, all indefatigable in their noble tasks. It was a different place when Damien came there, and made his great renunciation, and slept that first night under a tree amidst his rotting brethren: alone with pestilence; and looking forward (with what courage, with what pitiful sinkings of dread, God only knows) to a lifetime of dressing sores and stumps.

You will say, perhaps, I am too sensitive, that sights as painful abound in cancer hospitals and are confronted daily by doctors and nurses. I have long learned to admire and envy the doctors and the nurses. But there is no cancer hospital so large and populous as Kalawao and Kalaupapa; and in such a matter every fresh case, like every inch of length in the pipe of an organ, deepens the note of the impression; for what daunts the onlooker is that monstrous sum of human suffering by which he stands surrounded. Lastly, no doctor or nurse is called upon to enter once for all the doors of that gehenna; they do not say farewell, they need not abandon hope, on its sad threshold; they but go for a time to their high calling, and can look forward as they go to relief, to recreation, and to rest. But Damien shut to with his own hand the doors of his own sepulchre.

I shall now extract three passages from my diary at Kalawao.

A. "Damien is dead and already somewhat ungratefully remembered in the field of his labours and sufferings. 'He was a good man, but very officious,' says one. Another tells me he had fallen (as other priests so easily do) into something of the ways and habits of thought of a Kanaka; but he had the wit to recognise the fact, and the good sense to laugh at [over] it. A plain man it seems he was; I cannot find he was a popular."

B. "After Ragsdale's death" (Ragsdale was a famous Luna, or overseer, of the unruly settlement) "there followed a brief term of office by Father Damien which served only to publish the weakness of that noble man. He was rough in his ways, and he had no control. Authority was relaxed; Damien's life was threatened, and he was soon eager to resign."

C. "Of Damien I begin to have an idea. He seems to have been a man of the peasant class, certainly of the peasant type:

shrewd; ignorant and bigoted, yet with an open mind, and capable of receiving and digesting a reproof if it were bluntly administered; superbly generous in the least thing as well as in the greatest, and as ready to give his last shirt (although not without human grumbling) as he had been to sacrifice his life; essentially indiscreet and officious, which made him a troublesome colleague; domineering in all his ways, which made him incurably unpopular with the Kanakas, but yet destitute of real authority, so that his boys laughed at him and he must carry out his wishes by the means of bribes. He learned to have a mania for doctoring; and set up the Kanakas against the remedies of his regular rivals: perhaps (if anything matter at all in the treatment of such a disease) the worst thing that he did, and certainly the easiest. The best and worst of the man appear very plainly in his dealings with Mr. Chapman's money; he had originally laid it out" [intended to lay it out] "entirely for the benefit of Catholics, and even so not wisely, but after a long, plain talk, he admitted his error fully and revised the list. The sad state of the boys' home is in part the result of his lack of control; in part, of his own slovenly ways and false ideas of hygiene. Brother officials used to call it 'Damien's Chinatown.' 'Well,' they would say, 'your Chinatown keeps growing.' And he would laugh with perfect goodnature, and adhere to his errors with perfect obstinacy. So much I have gathered of truth about this plain, noble human brother and father of ours; his imperfections are the traits of his face, by which we know him for our fellow; his martyrdom and his example nothing can lessen or annul; and only a person here on the spot can properly appreciate their greatness."

I have set down these private passages, as you perceive, without correction; thanks to you, the public has them in their bluntness. They are almost a list of the man's faults, for it is rather these that I was seeking: with his virtues, with the heroic profile of his life, I and the world were already sufficiently acquainted. I was besides a little suspicious of Catholic testimony; in no ill sense, but merely because Damien's admirers and disciples were the least likely to be critical. I know you will be more suspicious still; and the facts set down above were one and all collected from the lips of Protestants who had opposed the father in his life. Yet I am strangely deceived, or they build up the image of a man, with all his weaknesses, essentially heroic, and alive with rugged honesty, generosity and mirth.

Take it for what it is, rough private jottings of the worst sides of Damien's character, collected from the lips of those who had laboured with and (in your own phrase) "knew the man"—though I question whether Damien would have said that he knew you. Take it, and observe with wonder how well you were served by your gossips, how ill by your intelligence and sympathy; in how many points of fact we are at one, and how widely our appreciations vary. There is something wrong here; either with you or me. It is possible, for instance, that you, who seem to have so many ears in Kalawao, had heard of the affair of Mr. Chapman's money, and were singly struck by Damien's intended wrong-doing. I was struck with that also, and set is fairly down; but I was struck much more by the fact that he had the honesty of mind to be convinced. I may here tell you that it was a long business; that one of his colleagues sat with him late into the night, multiplying arguments and accusations; that the father listened as usual with "perfect good-nature and perfect obstinacy;" but at the last, when he was persuaded —"Yes," said he, "I am very much obliged to you; you have done me a service; it would have been a theft." There are many (not Catholics merely) who require their heroes and saints to be infallible; to these the story will be painful; not to the true lovers, patrons, and servants of mankind.

And I take it, this is a type of our division; that you are one of those who have an eye for faults and failures; that you take a pleasure to find and publish them; and that, having found them, you make haste to forget the overvailing virtues and the real success which had alone introduced them to your knowledge. It is a dangerous frame of mind. That you may understand how dangerous, and into what a situation it has already brought you, we will (if you please) go hand-in-hand through the different phrases of your letter, and candidly examine each from the point of view of its truth, its appositeness, and its charity.

Damien was *coarse*.

It is very possible. You make us sorry for the lepers who had only a coarse old peasant for their friend and father. But you, who were so refined, why were you not there, to cheer them with the lights of culture? Or may I remind you that we have some reason to doubt if John the Baptist were genteel; and in the case of Peter, on whose career you doubtless dwell approvingly in the pulpit, no doubt at all he was a "coarse, headstrong" fisherman! Yet even in our Protestant Bibles Peter is called Saint.

Damien was *dirty*.

He was. Think of the poor lepers annoyed with this dirty comrade! But the clean Dr. Hyde was at his food in a fine house.

Damien was *headstrong*.

I believe you are right again; and I thank God for his strong head and heart.

Damien was *bigoted*.

I am not fond of bigots myself, because they are not fond of me. But what is meant by bigotry, that we should regard it as a blemish in a priest? Damien believed his own religion with the simplicity of a peasant or a child; as I would I could suppose that you do. For this, I wonder at him some way off; and had that been his only character, should have avoided him in life. But the point of interest in Damien, which has caused him to be so much talked about and made him at last the subject of your pen and mine, was that, in him, his bigotry, his intense and narrow faith, wrought potently for good, and strengthened him to be one of the world's heroes and exemplars.

Damien *was not sent to Molokai, but went there without orders.*

Is this a misreading? or do you really mean the words for blame? I have heard Christ, in the pulpits of our Church, held up for imitation on the ground that His sacrifice was voluntary. Does Dr. Hyde think otherwise?

Damien *did not stay at the settlement, etc.*

It is true he was allowed many indulgences. Am I to understand that you blame the father for profiting by these, or the officers for granting them? In either case, it is a mighty Spartan standard to issue from the house on Beretania Street; and I am convinced you will find yourself with few supporters.

Damien *had no hand in the reforms, etc.*

I think even you will admit that I have already been frank in my description of the man I am defending; but before I take you up on this head, I will be franker still and tell you that perhaps nowhere in the world can a man taste a more pleasurable sense of contrast than when he passes from Damien's "Chinatown" at Kalawao to the beautiful Bishop-Home at Kalaupapa. At this point, in my desire to make all fair for you, I will break my rule and adduce Catholic testimony. Here is a passage from my diary about my visit to the China-town, from which you will see how it is (even now) regarded by its own officials: "We went round all the dormitories, refec-tories, etc.—dark and dingy enough, with a superficial cleanliness, which he" [Mr. Dutton, the lay brother] "did not seek to defend. 'It is almost decent,' said he; 'the sisters will make that all right when we get them here.' " And yet I gathered it was already better since Damien was dead, and far better than when he was there alone and had his own (not always excellent) way. I have now come far enough to meet you on a common ground of fact; and I tell you that, to a mind not prejudiced by jealousy, all the reforms of the lazaretto, and even those which he most vigorously opposed, are properly the work of Damien. They are the evidence of his success; they are what his heroism provoked from the reluctant and the careless. Many were before him in the field; Mr. Meyer, for instance, of whose faithful work we hear too little. there have been many since; and some had more worldly wisdom, though none had more devotion, than our saint. Before his day, even you will confess, they had effected little. It was his part, by one striking act of martyrdom, to direct all men's eyes on that distressful country. At a blow, and with the price of his life, he made the place illustrious and public. And that, if you will consider largely, was the one reform needful; pregnant of all that should succeed. It brought money; it brought (best individual addition of them all) the sisters; it brought supervision, for public opinion and public interest landed with the man at Kalawao. If ever any man brought reforms, and died to bring them, it was he. There is not a clean cup or towel in the Bishop-Home, but dirty Damien washed it.

Damien *was not a pure man in his relations with women, etc.*

How do you know that? Is this the nature of the conversation in that house on Beretania Street which the cabman envied, driving past?—the racy details of the misconduct of the poor peasant priest, toiling under the cliffs of Molokai?

Many have visited the station before me; they seem not to have heard the rumour. When I was there I heard many shocking tales, for my informants were men speaking with the plainness of the laity; and I heard plenty of complaints of Damien. Why was this never mentioned? and how came it to you in the retirement of your clerical parlour?

But I must not even seem to deceive you. This scandal, when I read it in your letter, was not new to me. I had heard it once before; and I must tell you how. There came to Samoa a man from Honolulu; he, in a public-house on the beach, volunteered the statement that Damien had "contracted the disease from having connection with the female lepers"; and I find a joy in telling you how the report was welcomed in a public-house. A man sprang to his feet; I am not at liberty to give his name, but from what I heard I doubt if you would care to have him to dinner in Beretania Street. "You miserable little — —" (here is a word I dare not print, it would so shock your ears). "You miserable little — —," he cried, "if the story were a thousand times true, can't you see you are a million times a lower — — for daring to repeat it?" I wish it could be told of you that when the report reached you in your house, perhaps after family worship, you had found in your soul enough holy anger to receive it with the same expressions: ay, even with that one which I dare not print; it would not need to have been blotted away, like Uncle Toby's oath, by the tears of the recording angel; it would have been counted to you for your brightest righteousness. But you have deliberately chosen the part of the man from Honolulu, and you have played it with improvements of your own. The man from Honolulu— miserable, leering creature—communicated the tale to a rude knot of beach-combing drinkers in a public-house, where (I will so far agree with your temperance opinions) man is not always at his noblest; and the man from Honolulu had himself been drinking—drinking, we may charitably fancy, to excess. It was to your "Dear Brother, the Reverend H. B. Gage," that you chose to communicate the sickening story; and the blue ribbon which adorns your portly bosom forbids me to allow you the extenuating plea that you were drunk when it was done. Your "dear brother"—a brother indeed—made haste to deliver up your letter (as a means of grace, perhaps) to the religious papers; where, after many months, I found and read and wondered at it; and whence I have now reproduced it for the wonder of others. And you and your dear brother have, by this cycle of operations, built up a contrast very edifying to examine in detail. The man whom you would not care to have to dinner, on the one side; on the other, the Reverend Dr. Hyde and the Reverend H. B. Gage: the Apia bar-room, the Honolulu manse.

But I fear you scarce appreciate how you appear to your fellowmen; and to bring home to you, I will suppose your story to be true. I will suppose—and God forgive me for supposing it—that Damien faltered and stumbled in his narrow path of duty; I will suppose that, in the horror of his isolation, perhaps in the fever of incipient disease, he, who was doing so much more than he had sworn, failed in the letter of his priestly oath —he, who was so much a better man than either you or me, who did what we have never dreamed of daring—he too tasted of our common frailty. "O, Iago, the pity of it!" The least tender should be moved to tears; the most incredulous to prayer. And all that you could do was to pen your letter to the Reverend H. B. Gage!

Is it growing at all clear to you what a picture you have drawn of your own heart? I will try yet once again to make it clearer. You had a father: suppose this tale were about him, and some informant brought it to you, proof in hand: I am not making too high an estimate of your emotional nature when I suppose you would regret the circumstances? that you would feel the tale of frailty the more keenly since it shamed the author of your days? and that the last thing you would do would be to publish it in the religious press? Well, the man who tried to do what Damien did, is my father, and the father of the man in the Apia bar, and the father of all who love goodness; and he was your father too, if God had given you grace to see it.

V

The Elements of Discord: Foreign
from *A Footnote to History*

The huge majority of Samoans, like other god-fearing folk in other countries, are perfectly content with their own manners. And upon one condition, it is plain they might enjoy themselves far beyond the average of man. Seated in islands very rich in food, the idleness of the many idle would scarce matter; and the provinces might continue to bestow their names among rival pretenders, and fall into war and enjoy that awhile, and drop into peace and enjoy that, in a manner highly to be envied. But the condition—that they should be let alone— is no longer possible. More than a hundred years ago, and following closely on the heels of Cook, an irregular invasion of adventurers began to swarm about the isles of the Pacific. The seven sleepers of Polynesia stand, still but half aroused, in the midst of the century of competition. And the island races, comparable to a shopful of crockery launched upon the stream of time, now fall to make their desperate voyage among pots of brass and adamant.

Apia, the port and mart, is the seat of the political sickness of Samoa. At the foot of a peaked, woody mountain, the coast makes a deep indent, roughly semi-circular. In front the barrier reef is broken by the fresh water of the streams; if the swell be from the north, it enters almost without diminution; and the warships roll dizzily at their moorings, and along the fringeing coral which follows the configuration of the beach, the surf breaks with a continuous uproar. In wild weather, as the world knows, the roads are untenable. Along the whole shore, which is everywhere green and level and overlooked by inland mountaintops, the town lies drawn out in strings and clusters. The western horn is Mulinuu, the eastern, Matautu; and from one to the other of these extremes, I ask the reader to walk. He will find more of the history of Samoa spread before his eyes in that excursion, than has yet been collected in the blue-books or the white-books of the world. Mulinuu (where the walk is to begin) is a flat, wind-swept promontory, planted with palms, backed against a swamp of mangroves, and occupied by a rather miserable village. The reader is informed that this is the proper residence of the Samoan kings; he will be the more surprised to observe a board set up, and to read that this historic village is the property of the German firm. But these boards, which are among the commonest features of the landscape, may be rather taken to imply that the claim has been disputed. A little further east he skirts the stores, offices, and barracks of the firm itself. Thence he will pass through Matafele, the one really town-like portion of this long string of villages, by German bars and stores and the German consulate; and to reach the Catholic mission and cathedral standing by the mouth of a small river. The bridge which crosses here (bridge of Mulivai) is a frontier; behind is Matafele; beyond, Apia proper; behind, Germans are supreme; beyond, with but few exceptions, all is Anglo-Saxon. Here the reader will go forward past the stores of Mr. Moors (American) and Messrs. MacArthur (English); past the English mission, the office of the English newspaper, the English church, and the old American consulate, till he reaches the mouth of a larger river, the Vaisingano. Beyond, in Matautu, his way takes him in the shade of many trees and by scattered dwellings, and presently brings him beside a great range of offices, the place and the monument of a German who fought the German firm during his life. His house (now he is dead) remains pointed like a discharged cannon at the citadel of his old enemies. Fitly enough, it is at present leased and occupied by Englishmen. A little further, and the reader gains the eastern flanking angle of the bay, where stands the pilot-house and signal post, and whence he can see, on the line of the main coast of the island, the British and the new American consulates.

The course of his walk will have been enlivened by a considerable to and fro of pleasure and business. He will have encountered many varieties of whites,—sailors, merchants, clerks, priests, Protestant missionaries in their pith helmets, and the nondescript hangers-on of any island beach. And the sailors are sometimes in considerable force; but not the residents. He will think at times there are more signboards than men to own them. It may chance it is a full day in the harbour; he will then have seen all manner of ships, from men-of-war and deep-sea packets to the labour vessels of the German firm and the cockboat island schooner; and if he be of an arithmetical turn, he may calculate that there are more whites afloat in Apia bay than whites ashore in the whole Archipelago. On the other hand, he will have encountered all ranks of natives, chiefs and pastors in their scrupulous white clothes; perhaps the king himself, attended by guards in uniform; smiling policemen with their pewter stars; girls, women, crowds of cheerful children. And he will have asked himself with some surprise where these reside. Here and there, in the back yards of European establishments, he may have had a glimpse of a native house elbowed in a corner; but since he left Mulinuu, none on the beach where islanders prefer to live, scarce one on the line of street. The handful of whites have everything; the natives walk in a foreign town. A year ago, on a knoll behind a barroom, he might have observed a native house guarded by sentries and flown over by the standard of Samoa. He would then have been told it was the seat of government, driven (as I have to relate) over the Mulivai and from beyond the German town into the Anglo-Saxon. To-day, he will learn it has been carted back again to its old quarters. And he will think it significant that the king of the islands should be thus shuttled to and fro in his chief city at the nod of aliens. And then he will observe a feature more significant still: a house with some concourse of affairs, policemen and idlers hanging by, a man at a bank counter overhauling manifests, perhaps a trial proceeding in the front verandah, or perhaps the council breaking up in knots after a stormy sitting. And he will remember that he is in the Eleele Sa, the "Forbidden Soil" or Neutral Territory of the treaties; that the magistrates whom he has just seen trying native criminals is no officer of the native king's; and that this, the only port and place of business in the kingdom, collects and administers its own revenue for its own behoof by the hands of white councillors and under the supervision of white consuls. Let him go farther afield. He will find the roads almost everywhere to cease or to be made impassable by native pig-fences, bridges to be quite unknown, and houses of the whites to become at once a rare exception. Set aside the German plantations, and the frontier is sharp. At the boundary of the Eleele Sa, Europe ends, Samoa begins. Here, then, is a singular state of affairs: all the money, luxury, and business of the kingdom centered in one place; that place excepted from the native government and administered by whites for whites; and the whites themselves holding it not in common but in hostile camps, so that it lies between them like a bone between two dogs, each growling, each clutching his own end.

Should Apia ever choose a coat of arms, I have a motto

ready: "Enter Rumour painted full of tongues." The majority
of the natives do extremely little; the majority of the whites
are merchants with some four mails in the month, shopkeepers
with some ten or twenty customers a day, and gossip is the
common resource of all. The town hums to the day's news, and
the bars are crowded with amateur politicians. Some are office-
seekers, and earwig king and consul, and compass the fall of
officials, with an eye to salary. Some are humourists, delighted
with the pleasure of faction for itself. "I never saw so good a
place as this Apia," said one of these; "you can be in a new
conspiracy every day!" Many, on the other hand, are sincerely
concerned for the future of the country. The quarters are so
close and the scale is so small, that perhaps not any one can be
trusted always to preserve his temper. Everyone tells everything he knows; that is our country sickness. Nearly everyone
has been betrayed at times, and told a trifle more; the way our
sickness takes the predisposed. And the news flies, and the
tongues wag, and fists are shaken. Pot boil and cauldron
bubble!

Within the memory of man, the white people of Apia lay in
the worst squalor of degradation. They are now unspeakably
improved, both men and women. Today they must be called
a more than fairly respectable population, and a much more
than fairly intelligent. The whole would probably not fill the
ranks of even an English half-battalion, yet there are a surprising number above the average in sense, knowledge, and
manners. The trouble (for Samoa) is that they are all here after
a livelihood. Some are sharp practioners, some are famous
(justly or not) for foul play in business. Tales fly. One merchant
warns you against his neighbour; the neighbour on the first
occasion is found to return the compliment: each with a good
circumstantial story to the proof. There is so much copra in
the islands, and no more; a man's share of it is his share of

bread; and commerce, like politics, is here narrowed to a focus, shows its ugly side, and becomes as personal as fisticuffs. Close at their elbows, in all this contention, stands the native looking on. Like a child, his true analogue, he observes, apprehends, misapprehends, and is usually silent. As in a child, a considerable intemperance of speech is accompanied by some power of secrecy. News he publishes; his thoughts have often to be dug for. He looks on at the rude career of the dollar hunt, and wonders. He sees these men rolling in a luxury beyond the ambition of native kings; he hears them accused by each other of the meanest trickery; he knows some of them to be guilty; and what is he to think? He is strongly conscious of his own position as the common milk cow; and what is he to do? "Surely these white men on the beach are not great chiefs?" is a common question, perhaps asked with some design of flattering the person questioned. And one, stung by the last incident into an unusual flow of English, remarked to me: "I begin to be weary of white men on the beach."

But the true center of trouble, the head of the boil of which Samoa languishes, is the German firm. From the conditions of business, a great island house must ever be an inheritance of care; and it chances that the greatest still afoot has its chief seat in Apia bay, and has sunk the main part of its capital in the island of Upolu. When its founder, John Caesar Godeffroy, went bankrupt over Russian paper and Westphalian iron, his most considerable asset was found to be the South Sea business. This passed (I understand) through the hands of Baring Brothers in London, and is now run by a company rejoicing in the Gargantuan name of the *Deutsche Handels und Plantagen Geselschaft für Sud-See Inseln zu Hamburg*. This piece of literature is (in practice) shortened to the D. H. and P. G., the Old Firm, the German Firm, the Firm, and (among humourists) the Long Handle Firm. Even from the deck of an approaching ship, the island is seen to bear its signature—zones of cultivation showing in a more vivid tint of green on the dark vest of forest. The total area in use is near ten thousand acres. Hedges of fragrant lime enclose, broad avenues intersect them. You shall walk for hours in parks of palm tree alleys, regular, like soldiers on parade; in the recesses of the hills you may stumble on a mill-house, toiling and trembling there, fathoms deep in superincumbent forest. On the carpet of clean sward, troops of horses and herds of handsome cattle may be seen to browse; and to one accustomed to the rough luxuriance of the tropics, the appearance is of fairyland. The managers, many of them German sea-captains, are enthusiastic in their new employment. Experiment is continually afoot: coffee and cacao, both of excellent quality, are among the more recent outputs; and from one plantation quantities of pineapples are sent at a particular season to the Sydney markets. A hundred and fifty thousand pounds of English money, perhaps two hundred thousand, lie sunk in these magnificent estates. In estimating the expense of maintenance, quite a fleet of ships must be remembered, and a strong staff of captains, supercargoes, overseers, and clerks. These last mess together at a liberal board; the wages are high, and the staff is inspired with a strong and pleasing sentiment of loyalty to their employers.

Seven or eight hundred imported men and women toil for the company on contracts of three or of five years, and at a hypothetical wage of a few dollars in the month. I am now on a burning question: the labour traffic; and I shall ask permission in this place only to touch it with the tongs. Suffice it to say that in Queensland, Fiji, New Caledonia, and Hawaii it has been either suppressed or placed under close public supervision. In Samoa, where it still flourishes, there is no regulation of which the public receives any evidence; and the dirty linen of the firm, if there be any dirty, and if it be ever washed at all, is washed in private. This is unfortunate, if Germans would believe it. But they have no idea of publicity, keep their business to themselves, rather affect to "move in a mysterious way," and are naturally incensed by criticisms, which they consider hypocritical, from men who would import "labour" for themselves, if they could afford it, and would probably maltreat them if they dared. It is said the whip is very busy on some of the plantations; it is said that punitive extra-labour, by which the thrall's term of service is extended, has grown to be an abuse; and it is complained that, even where that term is out, much irregularity occurs in the repatriation of the discharged. To all this I can say nothing, good or bad. A certain number of the thralls, many of them wild negritos from the west, have taken to the bush, harbour there in a state partly bestial, or creep into the back quarters of the town to do a day's stealthy labour under the nose of their proprietors. Twelve were arrested one morning in my own boys' kitchen. Further in the bush, huts, small patches of cultivation, and smoking ovens, have been found by hunters. There are still three runaways in the woods of Tutuila, whither they escaped upon a raft. And the Samoans regard these dark-skinned rangers with extreme alarm; the fourth refugee in Tutuila was shot down (as I was told in that island) while carrying off the virgin of a village; and tales of cannibalism run round the country, and the natives shudder about the evening fire. For the Samoans are not cannibals, do not seem to remember any period when they were, and regard the practice with a disfavor equal to our own.

The firm is Gulliver among the Lilliputs; and it must not be forgotten, that while the small, independent traders are fighting for their own hand and inflamed with the usual jealousy against corporations, the Germans are inspired with a sense of the greatness of their affairs and interests. The thought of the money sunk, the sight of these costly and beautiful plantations menaced yearly by the returning forest, and the responsibility of administering with one hand so many conjunct fortunes, might well nerve the manager of such a company for desperate and questionable deeds. Upon this scale, commercial sharpness has an air of patriotism; and I can imagine the man, so far from higgling over the scourge for a few Solomon islanders, prepared to oppress rival firms, overthrow inconvenient monarchs, and let loose the dogs of war. Whatever he may decide, he will not want for backing. Every clerk will be eager to be up and strike a blow; and most Germans in the group, whatever they may babble of the firm over the walnuts and the wine, will rally round the national concern at the approach of difficulty. There are so few—I am ashamed to give their number, "it were to challenge contradiction—they are so few, and the amount of national capital buried at their feet is so vast, that we must not wonder if they seem oppressed with greatness and the sense of empire. Other whites take part in our babbles, while temper holds out, with a certain schoolboy entertainment. In the Germans alone, no trace of humour is to be observed, and their solemnity is accompanied by a touchiness often beyond belief. Patriotism flies in arms about a hen; and if you comment upon the colour of a Dutch umbrella, you have cast a stone against the German emperor. I give one instance, typical although extreme. One who had returned from Tutuila on the mail cutter complained of the vermin with which she is infested. He was suddenly and sharply brought to a stand. The ship of which he spoke, he was reminded, was a German ship.

John Caesar Godeffroy himself had never visited the islands; his sons and nephews came, indeed, but scarcely to reap laurels; and the mainspring and head-piece of this great concern, until death took him, was a certain remarkable man of the name of Theodore Weber. He was of an artful and commanding

character; in the smallest thing or the greatest, without fear
or scruple; equally able to affect, equally ready to adopt, the
most engaging politeness or the most imperious airs of
domination. It was he who did most damage to rival
traders; it was he who most harried the Samoans; and
yet I never met any one, white or native, who did not
respect his memory. All felt it was a gallant battle, and the
man a great fighter; and now when he is dead, and the war
seems to have gone against him, many can scarce remember,
without a kind of regret, how much devotion and audacity
have been spent in vain. His name still lives in the songs of
Samoa. One, that I have heard, tells of Misi Ueba and a biscuit
box—the suggesting incident being long since forgotten.
Another sings plaintively how all things, land and food and
property, pass progressively, as by a law of nature, into the
hands of Misi Ueba, and soon nothing will be left for Samoans.
This is an epitaph the man would have enjoyed.

At one period of his career, Weber combined the offices of
director of the firm and consul for the City of Hamburg. No
question but he then drove very hard. Germans admit that the
combination was unfortunate; and it was a German who
procured its overthrow. Captain Zembsch superseded him with
an imperial appointment, one still remembered in Samoa as
"the gentleman who acted justly." There was no house to be
found, and the new consul must take up his quarters at first
under the same roof with Weber. On several questions, in which
the firm was vitally interested, Zembsch embraced the contrary
opinion. Riding one day with an Englishman in Vailele plantation, he was startled by a burst of screaming, leaped from the
saddle, ran round a house, and found an overseer beating one
of the thralls. He punished the overseer, and, being a kindly
and perhaps not a very diplomatic man, talked high of what
he felt and what he might consider it his duty to forbid or to

enforce. The firm began to look askance at such a consul; and worse was behind. A number of deeds being brought to the consulate for registration, Zembsch detected certain transfers of land in which the date, the boundaries, the measure, and the consideration were all blank. He refused them with an indignation which he does not seem to have been able to keep to himself; and whether or not by his fault, some of these unfortunate documents b~came public. It was plain that the relations between the two flanks of the German invasion, the diplomatic and the commercial, were strained to bursting. But Weber was a man ill to conquer. Zembsch was recalled; and from that time forth, whether through influence at home, or by the solicitations of Weber on the spot, the German consulate has shown itself very apt to play the game of the German firm. That game, we may say, was twofold,—the first part even praiseworthy, the second at least natural. On the one part, they desired an efficient native administration, to open up the country and punish crime; they wished, on the other, to extend their own provinces and to curtail the dealings of their rivals. In the first, they had the jealous and diffident sympathy of all whites; in the second, they had all whites banded together against them for their lives and livelihoods. It was thus a game of *Beggar my Neighbour* between a large merchant and some small ones. Had it so remained, it would still have been a cut-throat quarrel. But when the consulate appeared to be concerned, when the war-ships of the German Empire were thought to fetch and carry for the firm, the rage of the independent traders broke beyond restraint. And, largely from the national touchiness and the intemperate speech of German clerks, this scramble among dollar hunters assumed the appearance of an inter-racial war.

The firm, with the indomitable Weber at its head and the consulate at its back—there has been the chief enemy of Samoa. No English reader can fail to be reminded of John Company;

and if the Germans appear to have been not so successful, we can only wonder that our own blunders and brutalities were less severely punished. Even on the field of Samoa, though German faults and aggressions make up the burthen of my story, they have been nowise alone. Three nations were engaged in this infinitesimal affray, and not one appears with credit. They figure but as the three ruffians of the elder playwrights. The States have the cleanest hands, and even theirs are not immaculate. It was an ambiguous business when a private American adventurer was landed with his pieces of artillery from an American warship, and became prime minister to the king. It is true (even if he were ever really supported) that he was soon dropped and had soon sold himself for money to the German firm. I will leave it to the reader whether this trait dignifies or not the wretched story. And the end of it spattered the credit alike of England and the States, when this man (the premier of a friendly sovereign) was kidnapped and deported, on the requisition of an American consul, by the captain of an English warship. I shall have to tell, as I proceed, of villages shelled on very trifling grounds by Germans; the like has been done of late years, though in a better quarrel, by ourselves of England. I shall have to tell how the Germans landed and shed blood at Fangalii; it was only in 1876 that we British had our own misconceived little massacre at Mulinuu. I shall have to tell how the Germans bludgeoned Malietoa with a sudden call for money; it was something of the suddenest that Sir Arthur Gordon himself, smarting under a sensible public affront, made and enforced a somewhat similar demand.

VI

Virginibus Puerisque, Part 1

With the single exception of Falstaff, all Shakespeare's characters are what we call marrying men. Mercutio, as he was own cousin to Benedick and Biron, would have come to the same end in the long run. Even Iago had a wife, and, what is far stranger, he was jealous. People like Jacques and the Fool in Lear, although we can hardly imagine they would ever marry, kept single out of a cynical humour or for a broken heart, and not, as we do nowadays, from a spirit of incredulity and preference for the single state. For that matter, if you turn to George Sand's French version of *As You like It* (and I think I can promise you will like it but little), you will find Jacques marries Celia just as Orlando marries Rosalind.

At least there seems to have been much less hesitation over marriage in Shakespeare's days; and what hesitation there was was of a laughing sort, and not much more serious, one way or the other, than that of Pan-urge. In modern comedies the heroes are mostly of Benedick's way of thinking, but twice as much in earnest, and not one quarter so confident. And I take this diffidence as a proof of how sincere their terror is. They know they are only human after all; they know what gins and pitfalls lie about their feet; and how the shadow of matrimony waits, resolute and awful, at the crossroads. They would wish to keep their liberty; but if that may not be, why, God's will be done!

"What, are you afraid of marriage?" asks Cécile, in *Maître Guerin.*

"*Oh, mon Dieu, non!*" replies Arthur; "I should take chloroform." They look forward to marriage much in the same way as they prepare themselves for death: each seems inevitable; each is a great Perhaps, and a leap into the dark, for which, when a man is in the blue devils, he has specially to harden his heart. That splendid scoundrel, Maxime de Trailles, took the news of marriages much as an old man hears the deaths of his contemporaries. "*C'est désespérant,*" he cried, throwing himself down in the armchair at Madame Schontz's; "*c'est désespérant, nous nous marions tou!*" Every marriage was like another grey hair on his head; and the jolly church bells seemed to taunt him with his fifty years and fair round belly.

The fact is, we are much more afraid of life than our ancestors, and cannot find it in our hearts either to marry or not to marry. Marriage is terrifying, but so is a cold and forlorn old age. The friendships of men are vastly agreeable, but they are insecure. You know all the time that one friend will marry and put you to the door; a second accept a situation in China, and become no more to you than a name, a reminiscence, and an occasional crossed letter, very laborious to read; a third will take up with some religious crotchet and treat you to sour looks thenceforward. So, in one way or another, life forces men apart and breaks up the goodly fellowships for ever. The very flexibility and ease which make men's friendships so agreeable while they endure, make them the easier to destroy and forget. And a man who has a few friends, or one who has a dozen (if there be any one so wealthy on this earth), cannot forget on how precarious a base his happiness reposes; and how by a stroke or two of fate—a death, a few light words, a piece of stamped paper, a woman's bright eyes—he may be left, in a month, destitute of all. Marriage is certainly a perilous remedy. Instead of on two or three, you stake your happiness on one life only. But still, as the bargain is more explicit and complete on your part, it is more so on the other; and you have not to fear so many contingencies; it is not every wind that can blow you from your anchorage; and so long as Death withholds his sickle, you will always have a friend at home. People who share a cell in the Bastille, or are thrown together on an uninhabited island, if they do not immediately fall to fisticuffs, will find some possible ground of compromise. They will learn each other's ways and humours, so as to know where they must go warily, and where they may lean their whole weight. The discretion of the first years becomes the settled habit of the last; and so, with wisdom and patience, two lives may grow indissolubly into one.

But marriage, if comfortable, is not at all heroic. It certainly narrows and damps the spirits of generous men. In marriage, a man becomes slack and selfish, and undergoes a fatty degeneration of his moral being. It is not only when Lydgate misallies himself with Rosamond Vincy, but when Ladislaw marries above him with Dorothea, that this may be exemplified. The air of the fireside withers out all the fine wildings of the husband's heart. He is so comfortable and happy that he begins to prefer comfort and happiness to everything else on earth, his wife included. Yesterday he would have shared his last shilling; to-day "his first duty is to his family," and is fulfilled in large measure by laying down vintages and husbanding the health of an invaluable parent. Twenty years ago this man was equally capable of crime or heroism; now he is fit for neither. His soul is asleep, and you may speak without constraint; you will not wake him. It is not for nothing that Don Quixote was a bachelor and Marcus Aurelius married ill. For women, there is less of this danger. Marriage is of so much use to a woman, opens out to her so much more of life, and puts her in the way of so much more freedom and usefulness, that, whether she marry ill or well, she can hardly miss some benefit. It is true, however, that some of the merriest and most genuine of women are old maids; and that those old maids, and wives who are unhappily married, have often most of the true motherly touch. And this would seem to show, even for women, some narrowing influence in comfortable married life. But the rule is none the less certain: if you wish the pick of men and women, take a good bachelor and a good wife.

I am often filled with wonder that so many marriages are passably successful, and so few come to open failure, the more so as I fail to understand the principle on which people regulate their choice. I see women marrying indiscriminately with staring burgesses and ferret-faced, white-eyed boys, and men dwelling in contentment with noisy scullions, or taking into their lives acidulous vestals. It is a common answer to say the good people marry because they fall in love; and of course you may use and misuse a word as much as you please, if you have the world along with you. But love is at least a somewhat hyperbolical expression for such lukewarm preference. It is not here, anyway, that Love employs his golden shafts; he cannot be said, with any fitness of language, to reign here and revel. Indeed, if this be love at all, it is plain the poets have been fooling with mankind since the foundation of the world. And you have only to look these happy couples in the face, to see they have never been in love, or in hate, or in any other high passion, all their days. When you see a dish of fruit at dessert, you sometimes set your affections upon one particular peach or nectarine, watch it with some anxiety as it comes round the table, and feel quite a sensible disappointment when it is taken by some one else. I have used the phrase "high passion." Well, I should say this was about as high a passion as generally leads to marriage. One husband hears after marriage that some poor fellow is dying of his wife's love.

"What a pity!" he exclaims; "you know I could so easily have got another!" And yet that is a very happy union. Or again: A young man was telling me the sweet story of his loves. "I like it well enough as long as her sisters are there," said this amorous swain; "but I don't know what to do when we're alone." Once more: A married lady was debating the subject with another lady. "You know, dear," said the first, "after ten years of marriage, if he is nothing else, your husband is always an old friend." "I have many old friends," returned the other, "but I prefer them to be nothing more." "Oh, perhaps I might *prefer* that also!" There is a common note in these three illustrations of the modern idyll; and it must be owned the god goes among us with a limping gait and blear eyes. You wonder whether it was so always; whether desire was always equally dull and spiritless, and possession equally cold. I cannot help fancying most people make, ere they marry, some such table of recommendations as Hannah Godwin wrote to her brother William anent her friend, Miss Gay. It is so charmingly comical, and so pat to the occasion, that I must quote a few phrases. "The young lady is in every sense formed to make one of your disposition really happy. She has a pleasing voice, with which she accompanies her musical instrument with judgment. She has an easy politeness in her manners, neither free nor reserved. She is a good housekeeper and a good economist, and yet of a generous disposition. As to her internal accomplishments, I have reason to speak still more highly of them: good sense without vanity, a penetrating judgment without a disposition to satire, with about as much religion as my William likes, struck me with a wish that she was my William's wife." That is about the tune: pleasing voice, moderate good looks, unimpeachable internal accomplishments after the style of the copy-book, with about as much religion as my William likes; and then, with all speed, to church.

To deal plainly, if they only married when they fell in love, most people would die unwed; and among the others there would be not a few tumultuous households. The Lion is the King of Beasts, but he is scarcely suitable for a domestic pet. In the same way, I suspect love is rather too violent a passion to make, in all cases, a good domestic sentiment. Like other violent excitements, it throws up not only what is best, but what is worst and smallest, in men's characters. Just as some people are malicious in drink, or brawling and virulent under the influence of religious feeling, some are moody, jealous, and exacting when they are in love, who are honest downright, good-hearted fellows enough in the everyday affairs and humours of the world.

How then, seeing we are driven to the hypothesis that people choose in comparatively cold blood, how is it they choose so well? One is almost tempted to hint that it does not much matter whom you marry; that, in fact, marriage is a subjective affection, and if you have made up your mind to it, and once talked yourself fairly over, you could "pull it through" with anybody. But even if we take matrimony at its lowest, even if we regard it as no more than a sort of friendship recognised by the police, there must be degrees in the freedom and sympathy realised, and some principle to guide simple folk in their selection. Now what should this principle be? Are there no more definite rules than are to be found in the Prayer-book? Law and religion forbid the bans on the ground of propinquity or consanguinity; society steps in to separate classes; and in all this most critical matter, has common sense, has wisdom, never a word to say? In the absence of more magisterial teaching, let us talk it over between friends: even a few guesses may be of interest to youths and maidens.

In all that concerns eating and drinking, company, climate, and ways of life, community of taste is to be sought for. It would be trying, for instance, to keep bed and board with an early riser or a vegetarian. In matters of art and intellect, I believe it is of no consequence. Certainly it is of none in the companionships of men, who will dine more readily with one who has a good heart, a good cellar, and a humorous tongue, than with another who shares all their favourite hobbies and is melancholy withal. If your wife likes Tupper, that is no reason why you should hang your head. She thinks with the majority, and has the courage of her opinions. I have always suspected public taste to be a mongrel product out of affectation by dogmatism; and felt sure, if you could only find an honest man of no special literary bent, he would tell you he thought much of Shakespeare bombastic and most absurd, and all of him written in very obscure English and wearisome to read. And not long ago I was able to lay by my lantern in content, for I found the honest man. He was a fellow of parts, quick, humorous, a clever painter, and with an eye for certain poetical effects of sea and ships. I am not much of a judge of that kind of thing, but a sketch of his comes before me sometimes at night. How strong, supple, and living the ship seems upon the billows! With what a dip and rake she shears the flying sea! I cannot fancy the man who saw this effect, and took it on the wing with so much force and spirit, was what you call commonplace in the last recesses of the heart. And yet he thought, and was not ashamed to have it known of him, that Ouida was better in every way than William Shakespeare. If there were more people of his honesty, this would be about the staple of lay criticism. It is not taste that is plentiful, but courage that is rare. And what have we in place? How many, who think no otherwise than the young painter, have we not heard disbursing second-hand hyperboles? Have you never

turned sick at heart, O best of critics! when some of your own
sweet adjectives were returned on you before a gaping audi-
ence? Enthusiasm about art is become a function of the
average female being, which she performs with precision and a
sort of haunting sprightliness, like an ingenious and well-
regulated machine. Sometimes, alas! the calmest man is carried
away in the torrent, bandies adjectives with the best, and out-
Herods Herod for some shameful moments. When you remember that, you will be tempted to put things strongly, and say
you will marry no one who is not like George the Second, and
cannot state openly a distaste for poetry and painting.

The word "facts" is, in some ways, crucial. I have spoken
with Jesuits and Plymouth Brethren, mathematicians and poets,
dogmatic republicans and dear old gentlemen in bird's-eye
neckcloths; and each understood the word "facts" in an occult
sense of his own. Try as I might, I could get no nearer the
principle of their division. What was essential to them, seemed
to me trivial or untrue. We could come to no compromise as
to what was, or what was not, important in the life of man.
Turn as we pleased, we all stood back to back in a big ring, and
saw another quarter of the heavens, with different mountaintops along the skyline and different constellations overhead.
We had each of us some whimsy in the brain, which we believed
more than anything else, and which discoloured all experience
to its own shade. How would you have people agree, when one
is deaf and the other blind? Now this is where there should
be community between man and wife. They should be agreed
on their catchword in *"facts of religion,"* or *"facts of science,"*
or *"society, my dear"*; for without such an agreement all intercourse is a painful strain upon the mind. "About as much
religion as my William likes," in short, that is what is necessary
to make a happy couple of any William and his spouse. For
there are differences which no habit nor affection can reconcile,

and the Bohemian must not inter-marry with the Pharisee. Imagine Consuelo as Mrs. Samuel Budgett, the wife of the successful merchant! The best of men and the best of women may sometimes live together all their lives, and, for want of some consent on fundamental questions, hold each other lost spirits to the end.

A certain sort of talent is almost indispensable for people who would spend years together and not bore themselves to death. But the talent, like the agreement, must be for and about life. To dwell happily together, they should be versed in the niceties of the heart, and born with a faculty for willing compromise. The woman must be talented as a woman, and it will not much matter although she is talented in nothing else. She must know her *métier de femme* and have a fine touch for the affections. And it is more important that a person should be a good gossip, and talk pleasantly and smartly of common friends and the thousand and one nothings of the day and hour, than that she should speak with the tongues of men and angels; for a while together by the fire, happens more frequently in marriage than the presence of a distinguished foreigner to dinner. That people should laugh over the same sort of jests, and have many a story of "grouse in the gun-room," many an old joke between them which time cannot wither nor custom stale, is a better preparation for life, by your leave, than many other things higher and better sounding in the world's ears. You could read Kant by yourself, if you wanted; but you must share a joke with someone else. You can forgive people who do not follow you through a philosophical disquisition; but to find your wife laughing when you had tears in your eyes, or staring when you were in a fit of laughter, would go some way towards a dissolution of the marriage.

I know a woman who, from some distaste or disability, could never so much as understand the meaning of the word politics, and has given up trying to distinguish Whigs from Tories; but take her on her own politics, ask her about other men or women and chicanery of everyday existence—the rubs, the tricks, the vanities on which life turns—and you will not find many more shrewd, trenchant, and humorous. Nay, to make plainer what I have in mind, this same woman has a share of the higher and more poetical understanding, frank interest in things for their own sake, and enduring astonishment at the most common. She is not to be deceived by custom, or made to think a mystery solved when it is repeated. I have heard her say she could wonder herself crazy over the human eyebrow. Now in a world where most of us walk very contentedly in the little lit circle of their own reason, and have to be reminded of what lies without by specious and clamant exceptions—earthquakes, eruptions of Vesuvius, banjos floating in mid-air at a séance, and the like—a mind so fresh and unsophisticated is no despicable gift. I will own I think it a better sort of mind than goes necessarily with the clearest views on public business. It will wash. It will find something to say at an odd moment. It has in it the spring of pleasant and quaint fancies. Whereas I can imagine myself yawning all night long until my jaws ached and the tears came into my eyes, although my companion on the other side of the hearth held the most enlightened opinions on the franchise or the ballot.

The question of professions, in as far as they regard marriage, was only interesting to women until of late days, but it touches all of us now. Certainly, if I could help it, I would never marry a wife who wrote. The practice of letters is miserably harassing to the mind; and after an hour or two's work, all the more human portion of the author is extinct; he will bully, backbite, and speak daggers. Music, I hear, is not much better. But painting, on the contrary, is often highly sedative; because so much of the labour, after your picture is once begun, is almost entirely manual, and of that skilled sort of manual labour which offers a continual series of successes, and so tickles a man, through his vanity, into good humour. Alas! in letters there is nothing of this sort. You may write as beautiful a hand as you will, you have always something else to think of, and cannot pause to notice your loops and flourishes; they are beside the mark, and the first law stationer could put you to the blush. Rousseau, indeed, made some account of penmanship, even made it a source of livelihood, when he copied out the *Héloise* for *dilettante* ladies; and therein showed that strange eccentric prudence which guided him among so many thousand follies and insanities. It would be well for all of the *genus irritabile* thus to add something of skilled labour to intangible brainwork. To find the right word is so doubtful a success and lies so near to failure, that there is no satisfaction in a year of it; but we all know when we have formed a letter perfectly; and a stupid artist, right or wrong, is almost equally certain he has found a right tone or a right colour, or made a dexterous stroke with his brush. And, again, painters may work out of doors; and the fresh air, the deliberate seasons, and the "tranquillising influence" of the green earth, counterbalance the fever of thought, and keep them cool, placable, and prosaic.

A ship captain is a good man to marry if it is a marriage of love, for absences are a good influence in love and keep it bright and delicate; but he is just the worst man if the feeling is more pedestrian, as habit is too frequently torn open and the solder has never time to set. Men who fish, botanise, work with the turning-lathe, or gather sea-weeds, will make admirable husbands; and a little amateur painting in water-colour shows the innocent and quiet mind. Those who have a few intimates are to be avoided; while those who swim loose, who have their hat in their hand all along the street, who can number an infinity of acquaintances and are not chargeable with any one friend, promise an easy disposition and no rival to the wife's influence. I will not say they are the best of men, but they are the stuff out of which adroit and capable women manufacture the best of husbands. It is to be noticed that those who have loved once or twice already are so much the better educated to a woman's hand; the bright boy of fiction is an odd and most uncomfortable mixture of shyness and coarseness, and needs a deal of civilising. Lastly (and this is, perhaps, the golden rule), no woman should marry a teetotaller, or a man who does not smoke. It is not for nothing that this "ignoble tabagie," as Michelet calls it, spreads over all the world. Michelet rails against it because it renders you happy apart from thought or work; to provident women this will seem no evil influence in married life. Whatever keeps a man in the front garden, whatever checks wandering fancy and all inordinate ambition, whatever makes for lounging and contentment, makes just so surely for domestic happiness.

These notes, if they amuse the reader at all, will probably amuse him more when he differs than when he agrees with them; at least they will do no harm, for nobody will follow my advice. But the last word is of more concern. Marriage is a step so grave and decisive that it attracts light-headed, variable men by its very awfulness. They have been so tried among the inconstant squalls and currents, so often sailed for islands in the air or lain becalmed with burning heart, that they will risk all for solid ground beneath their feet. Desperate pilots, they run their sea-sick, weary bark upon the dashing rocks. It seems as if marriage were the royal road through life, and realised, on the instant, what we have all dreamed on summer Sundays when the bells ring, or at night when we cannot sleep for the desire of living. They think it will sober and change them. Like those who join a brotherhood, they fancy it needs but an act to be out of the coil and clamour for ever. But this is a wile of the devil's. To the end, spring winds will sow disquietude, passing faces leave a regret behind them, and the whole world keep calling and calling in their ears. For marriage is like life in this—that it is a field of battle, and not a bed of roses.

VII

Talks and Talkers (First Paper)

"Sir, we had a good talk."—Johnson.

"As we must account for every idle word, so we must for every idle silence."—Franklin.

There can be no fairer ambition than to excel in talk; to be affable, gay, ready, clear and welcome; to have a fact, a thought, or an illustration, pat to every subject; and not only to cheer the flight of time among our intimates, but bear our part in that great international congress, always sitting, where public wrongs are first declared, public errors first corrected, and the course of public opinion shaped, day by day, a little nearer to the right. No measure comes before Parliament but it has been long ago prepared by the grand jury of the talkers; no book is written that has not been largely composed by their assistance. Literature in many of its branches is no other than the shadow of good talk; but the imitation falls far short of the original in life, freedom and effect. There are always two to a talk, giving and taking, comparing experience and according conclusions. Talk is fluid, tentative, continually "in further search and progress;" while written words remain fixed, become idols even to the writer, found wooden dogmatisms, and preserve flies of obvious error in the amber of the truth. Last and chief, while

97

literature, gagged with linsey-woolsey, can only deal with a fraction of the life of man, talk goes fancy free and may call a spade a spade. Talk has none of the freezing immunities of the pulpit. It cannot, even if it would, become merely aesthetic or merely classical like literature. A jest intervenes, the solemn humbug is dissolved in laughter, and speech runs forth out of the contemporary groove into the open fields of nature, cheery and cheering, like schoolboys out of school. And it is in talk alone that we can learn our period and ourselves. In short, the first duty of man is to speak; that is his chief business in this world; and talk, which is the harmonious speech of two or more, is by far the most accessible of pleasures. It costs nothing in money; it is all profit; it completes our education, founds and fosters our friendships, and can be enjoyed at any age and in almost any state of health.

The spice of life is battle; the friendliest relations are still a kind of contest; and if we would not forego all that is valuable in our lot, we must continually face some other person, eye to eye, and wrestle a fall whether in love or enmity. It is still by force of body or power of character or intellect, that we attain to worthy pleasures. Men and women contend for each other in the lists of love, like rival mesmerists; the active and adroit decide their challenges in the sports of the body; and the sedentary sit down to chess or conversation. All sluggish and pacific pleasures are, to the same degree, solitary and selfish; and every durable bond between human beings is founded in or heightened by some element of competition. Now, the relation that has the least root in matter is undoubtedly that airy one of friendship; and hence, I suppose, it is that good talk most commonly arises among friends. Talk is, indeed, both the scene and instrument of friendship. It is in talk alone that the friends can measure strength, and enjoy that amicable counter-assertion of personality which is the gauge of relations and the sport of life.

A good talk is not to be had for the asking. Humours must first be accorded in a kind of overture or prologue; hour, company and circumstance be suited; and then, at a fit juncture, the subject, the quarry of two heated minds, spring up like a deer out of the wood. Not that the talker has any of the hunter's pride, though he has all and more than all his ardour. The genuine artist follows the stream of conversation as an angler follows the windings of a brook, not dallying where he fails to "kill." He trusts implicitly to hazard; and he is rewarded by continual variety, continual pleasure, and those changing prospects of the truth that are the best of education. There is nothing in a subject, so called, that we should regard it as an idol, or follow it beyond the promptings of desire. Indeed, there are few subjects; and so far as they are truly talkable, more than the half of them may be reduced to three: that I am I, that you are you, and that there are other people dimly understood to be not quite the same as either. Wherever talk may range, it still runs half the time on these eternal lines. The theme being set, each plays on himself as on an instrument; asserts and justifies himself; ransacks his brain for instances and opinions, and brings them forth new-minted, to his own surprise and the admiration of his adversary. All natural talk is a festival of ostentation; and by the laws of the game each accepts and fans the vanity of the other. It is from that reason that we venture to lay ourselves so open, that we dare to be so warmly eloquent, and that we swell in each other's eyes to such a vast proportion. For talkers, once launched, begin to overflow the limits of their ordinary selves, tower up to the height of their secret pretensions, and give themselves out for the heroes, brave, pious, musical and wise, that in their most shining moments they aspire to be. So they weave for themselves with words and for a while inhabit a palace of delights, temple at once and theatre, where they fill the round of the world's dignities, and feast with the gods, exulting in Kudos. And when the talk is over, each goes his way, still flushed with vanity and admiration, still trailing clouds of glory; each declines from the height of his ideal orgie, not in a moment, but by slow declension. I remember, in the *entr'acte* of an afternoon performance, coming forth into the sunshine, in a beautiful green, gardened corner of a romantic city; and as I sat and smoked, the music moving in my blood, I seemed to sit there and evaporate *The Flying Dutchman* (for it was that I had been hearing) with a wonderful sense of life, warmth, well-being and pride; and the noises of the city, voices, bells and marching feet, fell together in my ears like a symphonious orchestra. In the same way, the excitement of a good talk lives for a long while after in the blood, the heart still hot within you, the brain still simmering, and the physical earth swimming around you with the colours of the sunset.

Natural talk, like ploughing, should turn up a large surface of life, rather than dig mines into geological strata. Masses of experience, anecdote, incident, crosslights, quotation, historical instances, the whole flotsam and jetsam of two minds forced in and in upon the matter in hand from every point of the compass, and from every degree of mental elevation and abasement—these are the material with which talk is fortified, the food on which the talkers thrive. Such argument as is proper to the exercise should still be brief and seizing. Talk should proceed by instances; by the apposite, not the expository. It should keep close along the lines of humanity, near the bosoms and businesses of men, at the level where history, fiction and experience intersect and illuminate each other. I am I, and You are You, with all my heart; but conceive how these lean propositions change and brighten when, instead of words, the actual you and I sit cheek by jowl, the spirit housed in the live body, and the very clothes uttering voices to corroborate the story in the face. Not less surprising is the change when we leave off to speak of generalities—the bad, the good, the miser, and all the characters of Theophrastus—and call up other men, by anecdote or instance, in their very trick and feature; or trading on a common knowledge, toss each other famous names, still glowing with the hues of life. Communication is no longer by words, but by the instancing of whole biographies, epics, systems of philosophy, and epochs of history, in bulk. That which is understood excels that which is spoken in quantity and quality alike; ideas thus figured and personified, change hands, as we may say, like coin; and the speakers imply without effort the most obscure and intricate thoughts. Strangers who have a large common ground of reading will, for this reason, come the sooner to the grapple of genuine converse. If they know Othello and Napoleon, Consuelo and Clarissa Harlowe, Vautrin and Steenie Steenson, they can leave generalities and begin at once to speak by figures.

Conduct and art are the two subjects that arise most frequently and that embrace the widest range of facts. A few pleasures bear discussion for their own sake, but only those which are most social or most radically human; and even these can only be discussed among their devotees. A technicality is always welcome to the expert, whether in athletics, art or law; I have heard the best kind of talk on technicalities from such rare and happy persons as both know and love their business. No human being ever spoke of scenery for above two minutes at a time, which makes me suspect we hear too much of it in literature. The weather is regarded as the very nadir and scoff of conversational topics. And yet the weather, the dramatic element in scenery, is far more tractable in language, and far more human both in import and suggestion than the stable features of the landscape. Sailors and shepherds, and the people generally of coast and mountain, talk well of it; and it is often excitingly presented in literature. But the tendency of all living talk draws it back and back into the common focus of humanity. Talk is a creature of the street and market-place, feeding on gossip; and its last resort is still in a discussion on morals. That is the heroic form of gossip; heroic in virtue of its high pretensions; but still gossip, because it turns on personalities. You can keep no men long, nor Scotchmen at all, off moral or theological discussion. These are to all the world what law is to lawyers; they are everybody's technicalities; the medium through which all consider life, and the dialect in which they express their judgments. I knew three young men who walked together daily for some two months in a solemn and beautiful forest and in cloudless summer weather; daily they talked with unabated zest, and yet scarce wandered that whole time beyond two subjects—theology and love. And perhaps neither a court of love nor an assembly of divines would have granted their premises or welcomed their conclusions.

Conclusions, indeed, are not often reached by talk any more than by private thinking. That is not the profit. The profit is in the exercise, and above all in the experience; for when we reason at large on any subject, we review our state and history in life. From time to time, however, and specially, I think, in talking art, talk becomes effective, conquering like war, widening the boundaries of knowledge like an exploration. A point arises; the question takes a problematical, a baffling, yet a likely air; the talkers begin to feel lively presentiments of some conclusion near at hand; towards this they strive with emulous ardour, each by his own path, and struggling for first utterance; and then one leaps upon the summit of that matter with a shout, and almost at the same moment the other is beside him; and behold they are agreed. Like enough, the progress is illusory, a mere cat's cradle having been wound and unwound out of words. But the sense of joint discovery is none the less giddy and inspiriting. And in the life of the talker such triumphs, though imaginary, are neither few nor far apart; they are attained with speed and pleasure, in the hour of mirth; and by the nature of the process, they are always worthily shared.

There is a certain attitude, combative at once and deferential, eager to fight yet most averse to quarrel, which marks out at once the talkable man. It is not eloquence, not fairness, not obstinacy, but a certain proportion of all of these that I love to encounter in my amicable adversaries. They must not be pontiffs holding doctrine, but huntsmen questing after elements of truth. Neither must they be boys to be instructed, but fellow-teachers with whom I may wrangle and agree on equal terms. We must reach some solution, some shadow of consent; for without that, eager talk becomes a torture. But we do not wish to reach it cheaply, or quickly, or without the tussle and effort wherein pleasure lies.

The very best talker, with me, is one whom I shall call Spring-Heel'd Jack. I say so, because I never knew any one who mingled so largely the possible ingredients of converse. In the Spanish proverb, the fourth man necessary to compound a salad, is a madman to mix it: Jack is that madman. I know not which is more remarkable; the insane lucidity of his conclusions, the humorous eloquence of his language, or his power of method, bringing the whole of life into the focus of the subject treated, mixing the conversational salad like a drunken god. He doubles like the serpent, changes and flashes like the shaken kaleidoscope, transmigrates bodily into the views of others, and so, in the twinkling of an eye and with a heady rapture, turns questions inside out and flings them empty before you on the ground, like a triumphant conjuror. It is my common practice when a piece of conduct puzzles me, to attack it in the presence of Jack with such grossness, such partiality and such wearing iteration, as at length shall spur him up in its defence. In a moment he transmigrates, dons the required character, and with moonstruck philosophy justifies the act in question. I can fancy nothing to compare with the vim of these impersonations, the strange scale of language, flying from Shakespeare to Kant, and from Kant to Major Dyngwell—

"As fast as a musician scatters sounds
Out of an instrument—"

the sudden, sweeping generalisations, the absurd irrelevant particularities, the wit, wisdom, folly, humour, eloquence and bathos, each startling in its kind, and yet all luminous in the admired disorder of their combination. A talker of a different calibre, though belonging to the same school, is Burly. Burly is a man of a great presence; he commands a larger atmosphere, gives the impression of a grosser mass of character than most men. It has been said of him that his presence could be felt in a room you entered blindfold; and the same, I think, has been said of other powerful constitutions condemned to much physical inaction. There is something boisterous and piratic in Burly's manner of talk which suits well enough with his impression. He will roar you down, he will bury his face in his hands, he will undergo passions of revolt and agony; and meanwhile his attitude of mind is really both conciliatory and receptive; and after Pistol has been out-Pistol'd, and the welkin rung for hours, you begin to perceive a certain subsidence in these spring torrents, points of agreement issue, and you end arm-in-arm, and in a glow of mutual admiration. The outcry only serves to make your final union the more unexpected and precious. Throughout there has been perfect sincerity, perfect intelligence, a desire to hear although not always to listen, and

an unaffected eagerness to meet concessions. You have, with
Burly, none of the dangers that attend debate with Spring-
Heel'd Jack; who may at any moment turn his powers of trans-
migration on yourself, create for you a view you never held,
and then furiously fall on you for holding it. These, at least,
are my two favourites, and both are loud, copious, intolerant
talkers. This argues that I myself am in the same category; for
if we love talking at all, we love a bright, fierce adversary, who
will hold his ground, foot by foot, in much our own manner,
sell his attention dearly, and give us our full measure of the
dust and exertion of battle. Both these men can be beat from a
position, but it takes six hours to do it; a high and hard
adventure, worth attempting. With both you can pass days in
an enchanted country of the mind, with people, scenery and
manners of its own; live a life apart, more arduous, active and
glowing than any real existence; and come forth again when
the talk is over, as out of a theatre or a dream, to find the east
wind still blowing and the chimney-pots of the old battered
city still around you. Jack has the far finer mind, Burly the
far more honest; Jack gives us the animated poetry, Burly the
romantic prose, of similar themes; the one glances high like
a meteor and makes a light in darkness; the other, with many
changing hues of fire, burns at the sea-level, like a conflagration;
but both have the same humour and artistic interests, the same
unquenched ardour in pursuit, the same gusts of talk and
thunderclaps of contradiction.

Cockshot[1] is a different article, but vastly entertaining, and
has been meat and drink to me for many a long evening. His
manner is dry, brisk and pertinacious, and the choice of words
not much. The point about him is his extraordinary readiness
and spirit. You can propound nothing but he has either a
theory about it ready-made, or will have one instantly on the

[1] The late Fleeming Jenkin.

stocks, and proceed to lay its timbers and launch it in your presence. "Let me see," he will say. "Give me a moment. I should have some theory for that." A blither spectacle than the vigour with which he sets about the task, it were hard to fancy. He is possessed by a demoniac energy, welding the elements for his life, and bending ideas, as an athlete bends a horseshoe, with a visible and lively effort. He has, in theorising, a compass, an art; what I would call the synthetic gusto; something of a Herbert Spencer, who should see the fun of the thing. You are not bound, and no more is he, to place your faith in these brand-new opinions. But some of them are right enough, durable even for life; and the poorest serve for a cock-shy—as when idle people, after picnics, float a bottle on a pond and have an hour's diversion ere it sinks. Whichever they are, serious opinions or humours of the moment, he still defends his ventures with indefatigable wit and spirit, hitting savagely himself, but taking punishment like a man. He knows and never forgets that people talk, first of all, for the sake of talking; conducts himself in the ring, to use the old slang, like a thorough "glutton," and honesty enjoys a telling facer from his adversary. Cockshot is bottled effervescency, the sworn foe of sleep. Three-in-the-morning Cockshot, says a victim. His talk is like the driest of all imaginable dry champagnes. Sleight of hand and inimitable quickness are the qualities by which he lives. Athelred, on the other hand, presents you with the spectacle of a sincere and somewhat slow nature thinking aloud. He is the most unready man I ever knew to shine in conversation. You may see him sometimes wrestle with a refractory jest for a minute or two together, and perhaps fail to throw it in the end. And there is something singularly engaging, often instructive, in the simplicity with which he thus exposes the process as well as the result, the works as well as the dial of the clock. Withal he has his hours of inspiration. Apt words come to him as if by accident, and, coming from deeper down, they smack the more personally, they have the more of fine old crusted humanity, rich in sediment and humour. There are sayings of his in which he has stamped himself into the very grain of the language; you would think he must have worn the words next his skin and slept with them. Yet it is not as a sayer of particular good things that Athelred is most to be regarded, rather as the stalwart woodman of thought. I have pulled on a light cord often enough, while he has been wielding the broad-axe; and between us, on this unequal division, many a specious fallacy has fallen. I have known him to battle the same question night after night for years, keeping it in the reign of talk, constantly applying it and re-applying it to life with humorous or grave intention, and all the while, never hurrying, nor flagging, nor taking an unfair advantage of the facts. Jack at a given moment, when arising, as it were, from the tripod, can be more radiantly just to those from whom he differs; but then the tenor of his thoughts is even calumnious; while Athelred, slower to forge excuses, is yet slower to condemn, and sits over the welter of the world, vacillating but still judicial, and still faithfully contending with his doubts.

Both the last talkers deal much in points of conduct and religion studied in the "dry light" of prose. Indirectly and as if against his will the same elements from time to time appear in the troubled and poetic talk of Opalstein. His various and exotic knowledge, complete although unready sympathies, and fine, full, discriminative flow of language, fit him out to be the best of talkers; so perhaps he is with some, not *quite* with me— *proxime accessit*, I should say. He sings the praises of the earth and the arts, flowers and jewels, wine and music, in a moonlight, serenading manner, as to the light guitar; even wisdom comes from his tongue like singing; no one is, indeed, more tuneful in the upper notes. But even while he sings the song of the Sirens, he still hearkens to the barking of the Sphinx. Jarring Byronic notes interrupt the flow of his Horatian humours. His mirth has something of the tragedy of the world for its perpetual background; and he feasts like Don Giovanni to a double orchestra, one lightly sounding for the dance, one pealing Beethoven in the distance. He is not truly reconciled either with life or with himself; and this instant war in his members sometimes divides the man's attention. He does not always, perhaps not often, frankly surrender himself in conversation. He brings into the talk other thoughts than those which he expresses; you are conscious that he keeps an eye on something else, that he does not shake off the world, nor quite forget himself. Hence arise occasional disappointments; even an occasional unfairness for his companions, who find themselves one day giving too much, and the next, when they are wary out of season, giving perhaps too little. Purcel is in another class from any I have mentioned. He is no debater, but appears in conversation, as occasion rises, in two distinct characters, one of which I admire and fear, and the other love. In the first, he is radiantly civil and rather silent, sits on a high, courtly hilltop, and from that vantage-ground drops you his remarks like favours. He seems not to share in our sublunary contentions; he wears no sign of interest; when on a sudden there falls in a crystal of wit, so polished that the dull do not perceive it, but so right that the sensitive are silenced. True talk should have more body and blood, should be louder, vainer and more declaratory of the man; the true talker should not hold so steady an advantage over whom he speaks with; and that is one reason out of a score why I prefer my Purcel in his second character, when he unbends into a strain of graceful gossip, singing like the fireside kettle. In these moods he has an elegant homeliness that rings of the true Queen Anne. I know another person who attains, in his moments, to the insolence of a Restoration comedy, speaking, I declare, as Congreve wrote; but that is a sport of nature, and scarce falls under the rubric, for there is none, alas! to give him answer.

One last remark occurs: It is the mark of genuine conversation that the sayings can scarce be quoted with their full effect beyond the circle of common friends. To have their proper weight they should appear in a biography, and with the portrait of the speaker. Good talk is dramatic; it is like an impromptu piece of acting where each should represent himself to the greatest advantage; and that is the best kind of talk where each speaker is most fully and candidly himself, and where, if you were to shift the speeches round from one to another, there would be the greatest loss in significance and perspicuity. It is for this reason that talk depends so wholly on our company. We should like to introduce Falstaff and Mercutio, or Falstaff and Sir Toby; but Falstaff in talk with Cordelia seems even painful. Most of us, by the Protean quality of man, can talk to some degree with all; but the true talk, that strikes out all the slumbering best of us, comes only with the peculiar brethren of our spirits, is founded as deep as love in the constitution of our being, and is a thing to relish with all our energy, while yet we have it, and to be grateful forever.

VIII

The Philosophy of Umbrellas

It is wonderful to think what a turn has been given to our whole Society by the fact that we live under the sign of Aquarius,—that our climate is essentially wet. A mere arbitrary distinction, like the walking-swords of yore, might have remained the symbol of foresight and respectability, had not the raw mists and dropping showers of our island pointed the inclination of Society to another exponent of those virtues. A ribbon of the Legion of Honour or a string of medals may prove a person's courage; a title may prove his birth; a professorial chair his study and acquirement; but it is the habitual carriage of the umbrella that is the stamp of Respectability. The umbrella has become the acknowledged index of social position.

Robinson Crusoe presents us with a touching instance of the hankering after them inherent in the civilised and educated mind. To the superficial, the hot suns of Juan Fernandez may sufficiently account for his quaint choice of a luxury; but surely one who had borne the hard labour of a seaman under the tropics for all these years could have supported an excursion after goats or a peaceful *constitutional* arm in arm with the nude Friday. No, it was not this: the memory of a vanished respecta-

---

[1] "This paper was written in collaboration with James Walter Ferrier, and if reprinted this is to be stated, though his principal collaboration was to lie back in an easy-chair and laugh."—(R.L.S., Oct. 25, 1894.)

bility called for some outward manifestation, and the result was—an umbrella. A pious castaway might have rigged up a belfry and solaced his Sunday mornings with the mimicry of church bells; but Crusoe was rather a moralist than a pietist, and his leaf-umbrella is as fine an example of the civilised mind striving to express itself under adverse circumstances as we have ever met with.

It is not for nothing, either, that the umbrella has become the very foremost badge of modern civilisation—the Urim and Thummim of respectability. Its pregnant symbolism has taken its rise in the most natural manner. Consider, for a moment, when umbrellas were first introduced into this country, what manner of men would use them, and what class would adhere to the useless but ornamental cane. The first, without doubt, would be the hypochondriacal, out of solicitude for their health, or the frugal, out of care for their raiment; the second, it is equally plain, would include the fop, the fool, and the Bobadil. Any one acquainted with the growth of Society, and knowing out of what small seeds of cause are produced great revolutions and wholly new conditions of intercourse, sees from this simple thought how the carriage of an umbrella came to indicate frugality, judicious regard for bodily welfare, and scorn for mere outward adornment, and, in one word, all those homely and solid virtues implied in the term RESPECTABILITY. Not that the umbrella's costliness has nothing to do with its great influence. Its possession, besides symbolising (as we have already indicated) the change from wild Esau to plain Jacob dwelling in tents, implies a certain comfortable provision of fortune. It is not every one that can expose twenty-six shillings' worth of property to so many chances of loss and theft. So strongly do we feel on this point, indeed, that we are almost inclined to consider all who possess really well-conditioned umbrellas as worthy of the Franchise. They have a qualification standing in their lobbies; they carry a sufficient stake in the common-weal below their arm. One who bears with him an umbrella—such a complicated structure of whale-bone, of silk, and of cane, that it becomes a very microcosm of modern industry—is necessarily a man of peace. A half-crown cane may be applied to an offender's head on a very moderate provocation; but a six-and-twenty shilling silk is a possession too precious to be adventured in the shock of war.

These are but a few glances at how umbrellas (in the general) came to their present high estate. But the true Umbrella-Philosopher meets with far stranger applications as he goes about the streets.

Umbrellas, like faces, acquire a certain sympathy with the individual who carries them: indeed, they are far more capable of betraying his trust; for whereas a face is given to us so far ready made, and all our power over it is in frowning, and laughing, and grimacing, during the first three or four decades of life, each umbrella is selected from a whole shopful, as being most consonant to the purchaser's disposition. An undoubted power of diagnosis rests with the practised Umbrella-Philosopher. O you who lisp, and amble, and change the fashion of your countenances—you who conceal all these, how little do you think that you left a proof of your weakness in our umbrella-stand—that even now, as you shake out the folds to meet the thickening snow, we read in its ivory handle the outward and visible sign of your snobbery, or from the exposed gingham of its cover detect, through coat and waistcoat, the hidden hypocrisy of the "dickey"! But alas! even the umbrella is no certain criterion. The falsity and the folly of the human race have degraded that graceful symbol to the ends of dishonesty; and while some umbrellas, from carelessness in selection, are not strikingly characteristic (for it is only in what a man loves that he displays his real nature), others, from certain prudential motives, are chosen directly opposite to the person's disposition. A mendacious umbrella is a sign of great moral degradation. Hypocrisy naturally shelters itself below a silk; while the fast youth goes to visit his religious friends armed with the decent and reputable gingham. May it not be said of the bearers of these inappropriate umbrellas that they go about the streets "with a lie in their right hand"?

The king of Siam, as we read, besides having a graduated social scale of umbrellas (which was a good thing), prevented the great bulk of his subjects from having any at all, which was certainly a bad thing. We should be sorry to believe that this Eastern legislator was a fool—the idea of an aristocracy of umbrellas is too philosophic to have originated in a nobody,—and we have accordingly taken exceeding pains to find out the reason of this harsh restriction. We think we have succeeded; but, while admiring the principle at which he aimed, and while cordially recognising in the Siamese potentate the only man before ourselves who had taken a real grasp of the umbrella, we must be allowed to point out how unphilosophically the great man acted in this particular. His object, plainly, was to prevent any unworthy persons from bearing the sacred symbol of domestic virtues. We cannot excuse his limiting these virtues to the circle of his court. We must only remember that such was the feeling of the age in which he lived. Liberalism had not yet raised the war-cry of the working classes. But here was his mistake: it was a needless regulation. Except in a very few cases of hypocrisy joined to a powerful intellect, men, not by nature umbrellarians, have tried again and again to become so by art, and yet have failed—have expended their patrimony in the purchase of umbrella after umbrella, and yet have systematically lost them, and have finally, with contrite spirits and shrunken purses, given up their vain struggle, and relied on theft and borrowing for the remainder of their lives. This is the most remarkable fact that we have had occasion to notice; and yet we challenge the candid reader to call it in question. Now, as there cannot be any moral selection in a mere dead piece of furniture—as the umbrella cannot be supposed to have an affinity for individual men equal and reciprocal to that which men certainly feel towards individual umbrellas,—we took the trouble of consulting a scientific friend as to whether there was any possible physical explanation of the phenomenon. He was unable to supply a plausible theory, or even hypothesis; but we extract from his letter the following interesting passage relative to the physical peculiarities of umbrellas: "Not the least important, and by far the most curious property of the umbrella, is the energy which it displays in affecting the atmospheric strata. There is no fact in meteorology better established—indeed, it is almost the only one on which meteorologists are agreed—than that the carriage of an umbrella produces desiccation of the air; while if it be left at home, aqueous vapour is largely produced, and is soon deposited in the form of rain. "No theory," my friend continues, "competent to explain this hygrometric law has yet been given (as far as I am aware) by Herschel, Dove, Glaisher, Tait, Buchan, or any other writer; nor do I pretend to supply the defect. I venture, however, to throw out the conjecture that it will be ultimately found to belong to the same class of natural laws as that agreeable to which a slice of toast always descends with the buttered surface downwards."

But it is time to draw to a close. We could expatiate much longer upon this topic, but want of space constrains us to leave unfinished these few desultory remarks—slender contributions towards a subject which has fallen sadly backwards, and which, we grieve to say, was better understood by the king of Siam in 1686 than by all the philosophers of to-day. If, however, we have awakened in any rational mind an interest in the symbolism of umbrellas—in any generous heart a more complete sympathy with the dumb companion of his daily walk,—or in any grasping spirit a pure notion of respectability strong enough to make him expend his six-and-twenty shillings—we shall have deserved well of the world, to say nothing of the many industrious persons employed in the manufacture of the article.

I X

Letters

To Charles Baxter

17 Heriot Row, Edinburgh,
Sunday, February 2, 1873.

My Dear Baxter—

The thunderbolt has fallen with a vengeance now. On Friday night after leaving you, in the course of conversation, my father put me one or two questions as to beliefs, which I candidly answered. I really hate all lying so much now—a new-found honesty that has somehow come out of my late illness—that I could not so much as hesitate at the time; but if I had foreseen the real hell of everything since, I think I should have lied, as I have done so often before. I so far thought of my father, but I had forgotten my mother. And now! they are both ill, both silent, both as down in the mouth as if—I can find no simile. You may fancy how happy it is for me. If it were not too late, I think I could almost find it in my heart to retract, but it is too late; and again, am I to live my whole life as one falsehood? Of course, it is rougher than hell! upon my father, but can I help it? They don't see either that my game is not the light-hearted scoffer; that I am not (as they call me) a careless infidel. I believe as much as they do, only generally in the inverse ratio: I am, I think, as honest as they can be in what I hold. I have not come hastily to my views. I reserve (as I told them) many points until I acquire fuller information, and do not think I am thus justly to be called "horrible atheist."

Now, what is to take place? What a curse I am to my parents! O Lord, what a pleasant thing it is to have just damned the happiness of (probably) the only two people who care a damn about you in the world!

What is my life to be at this rate? What, you rascal? Answer —I have a pistol at your throat. If all that I hold true and most desire to spread is to be such death, and worse than death, in the eyes of my father and mother, what the devil am I to do?

Here is a good heavy cross with a vengeance, and all rough with rusty nails that tear your fingers, only it is not I that have to carry it alone; I hold the light end, but the heavy burden falls on these two.

Don't—I don't know what I was going to say. I am an abject idiot, which, all things considered, is not remarkable.—Ever your affectionate and horrible atheist,

R. L. Stevenson.

To Thomas Stevenson

Paris
February 15, 1878.

My Dear Father—

A thought has come into my head which I think would interest you. Christianity is, among other things, a very wise, noble, and strange doctrine of life. Nothing is so difficult to specify as the position it occupies with regard to asceticism. It is not ascetic. Christ was of all doctors (if you will let me use the word) one of the least ascetic. And yet there is a theory of living in the Gospels which is curiously indefinable, and leans towards asceticism on one side, although it leans away from it on the other. In fact, asceticism is used therein as a means, not as an end. The wisdom of this world consists in making oneself very little in order to avoid many knocks; in preferring others, in order that even when we lose, we shall find some pleasure in the event; in putting our desires outside of ourselves, in another ship, so to speak, so that, when the worst happens, there will be something left. You see, I speak of it as a doctrine of life, and as a wisdom for this world. People must be themselves, I suppose. I feel every day as if religion had a greater interest for me; but that interest is still centred on the little rough-and-tumble world in which our fortunes are cast for the moment. I cannot transfer my interests, not even my religious interest, to any different sphere . . . I have had some sharp lessons and some very acute sufferings in these last seven-and-twenty years—more even than you would guess. I begin to grow an old man; a little sharp, I fear, and a little close and unfriendly; but still I have a good heart, and believe in myself and my fellow-men and the God who made us all. . . . There are not many sadder people in this world, perhaps, than I. I have my eye on a sickbed; I have written letters to-day that it hurt me to write, and I fear will hurt others to receive; I am lonely and sick out of heart. Well, I still hope; I still believe; I still see the good in the inch, and cling to it. It is not much, perhaps, but it is always something.

I find I have wandered a thousand miles from what I meant. It was this: of all passages bearing on Christianity in that form of a worldly wisdom, the most Christian, and so to speak, the key of the whole position, is the Christian doctrine of revenge. And it appears that this came into the world through Paul! There is a fact for you. It was to speak of this that I began this letter; but I have got into deep seas and must go on.

There is a fine text in the Bible, I don't know where, to the effect that all things work together for good to those who love the Lord. Strange as it may seem to you, everything has been, in one way or the other, bringing me a little nearer to what I think you would like me to be. 'Tis a strange world, indeed, but there is a manifest God for those who care to look for him.

This is a very solemn letter for my surroundings in this busy café; but I had it on my heart to write it; and, indeed, I was out of the humour for anything lighter.

Ever your affectionate son,

Robert Louis Stevenson.

P.S.—

While I am writing gravely, let me say one word more. I have taken a step towards more intimate relations with you. But don't expect too much of me. Try to take me as I am. This is a rare moment, and I have profited by it; but take it as a rare moment. Usually I hate to speak of what I really feel, to that extent that when I find myself cornered, I have a tendency to say the reverse.

R. L. S.

To Mrs. Thomas Stevenson

Christmas Sermon

Hotel Belvedere, Davos
December 26, 1880.

My Dear Mother—

I was very tired yesterday and could not write; tobogganed so furiously all morning; we had a delightful day, crowned by an incredible dinner—more courses than I have fingers on my hands. Your letter arrived duly at night, and I thank you for it as I should. You need not suppose I am at all insensible to my father's extraordinary kindness about this book; he is a brick; I vote for him freely.

. . . The assurance you speak of is what we all ought to have, and might have, and should not consent to live without. That people do not have it more than they do is, I believe, because persons speak so much in large-drawn theological similitudes, and won't say out what they mean about life, and man, and God, in fair and square human language. I wonder if you or my father ever thought of the obscurities that lie upon human duty from the negative form in which the Ten Commandments are stated, or of how Christ was so continually similitudes, and won't say out what they mean about life, and "Thou shalt" is the law of God. It was this that seems meant in the phrase that "not one jot nor tittle of the law should pass." But what led me to the remark is this: A kind of black, angry look goes with that statement of the law of negatives. "To love one's neighbour as oneself" is certainly much harder, but states life so much more actively, gladly, and kindly, that you can begin to see some pleasure in it; and till you can see pleasure in these hard choices and bitter necessities, where is there any Good News to men? It is much more important to do right than not to do wrong; further, the one is possible, the other has always been and will ever be impossible; and the faithful design to do right is accepted by God; that seems to me to be the Gospel, and that was how Christ delivered us from the Law. After people are told that, surely they might hear more encouraging sermons. To blow the trumpet for good would seem the Parson's business; and since it is not in our own strength, but by faith and perseverance (no account made of slips), that we are to run the race, I do not see where they get the material for their gloomy discourses. Faith is not to believe the Bible, but to believe in God; if you believe in God (or, for it's the same thing, have that assurance you speak about), where is there any more room for terror? There are only three possible attitudes—Optimism, which has gone to smash; Pessimism, which is on the rising hand, and very popular with many clergymen who seem to think they are Christians; and this Faith, which is the Gospel. Once you hold the last, it is your business (1) to find out what is right in any given case, and (2) to try to do it; if you fail in the last, that is by commission, Christ tells you to hope; if you fail in the first, that is by omission, his picture of the last day gives you but a black look-out. The whole necessary morality is kindness; and it should spring of itself, from the one fundamental doctrine, Faith. If you are sure that God, in the long run, means kindness by you, you should be happy; and if happy, surely you should be kind.

I beg your pardon for this long discourse; it is not all right, of course, but I am sure there is something in it. One thing I have not got clearly; that about the omission and the commission; but there is truth somewhere about it, and I have no time to clear it just now. Do you know, you have had about a Cornhill page of sermon? It is, however, true.

Lloyd heard with dismay Fanny was not going to give me a present; so F. and I had to go and buy things for ourselves, and go through a representation of surprise when they were presented next morning. It gave us both quite a Santa Claus feeling on Xmas Eve to see him so excited and hopeful; I enjoyed it hugely—

Your affectionate son,

Robert Louis Stevenson.

To the Rev. Dr. Charteris

Saranac Lake, Adirondacks
New York, U.S.A.
Spring, 1888.

My Dear Dr. Charteris—

The funeral letter, your notes, and many other things, are reserved for a book, *Memorials of a Scottish Family,* if ever I can find time and opportunity. I wish I could throw off all else and sit down to it to-day. Yes, my father was a "distinctly religious man," but not a pious. The distinction painfully and pleasurable recalls old conflicts; it used to be my great gun—and you, who suffered for the whole Church, know how needful it was to have some reserve artillery! His sentiments were tragic; he was a tragic thinker. Now, granted that life is tragic to the marrow, it seems the proper function of religion to make us accept and serve in that tragedy, as officers in that other and comparable one of war. Service is the word, active service, in the military sense; and the religious man—I beg pardon, the pious man—is he who has a military joy in duty—not he who weeps over the wounded. We can do no more than try to do our best. Really, I am the grandson of the manse—I preach you a kind of sermon. Box the brat's ears!

My mother—to pass to matters more within my competence —finely enjoys herself. The new country, some new friends we have made, the interesting experiment of this climate—which (at least) is tragic—all have done her good. I have myself passed a better winter than for years, and now that it is nearly over have some diffident hopes of doing well in the summer and "eating a little more air" than usual.

I thank you for the trouble you are taking, and my mother joins with me in kindest regards to yourself and Mrs. Charteris—

Yours very truly,
Robert Louis Stevenson.

To T. W. Dover

Vailima Plantation,
Upolu, Samoa
June 20, 1892.

Sir—

In reply to your very interesting letter, I cannot fairly say
that I have ever been poor, or known what it was to want a
meal. I have been reduced, however, to a very small sum of
money, with no apparent prospect of increasing it; and at that
time I reduced myself to practically one meal a day, with the
most disgusting consequences to my health. At this time I
lodged in the house of a working-man, and associated much
with others. At the same time, from my youth up, I have always
been a good deal and rather intimately thrown among the
working-classes, partly as a civil engineer in out-of-the-way
places, partly from a strong and, I hope, not ill-favoured sentiment of curiosity. But the place where, perhaps, I was most
struck with the fact upon which you comment was the house of
a friend, who was exceedingly poor, in fact, I may say destitute,
and who lived in the attic of a very tall house entirely inhabited
by persons in varying stages of poverty. As he was also in ill-
health, I made a habit of passing my afternoon with him, and
when there it was my part to answer the door. The steady procession of people begging, and the expectant and confident
manner in which they presented themselves, struck me more
and more daily; and I could not but remember with surprise
that though my father lived but a few streets away in a fine
house, beggars scarce came to the door once a fortnight or a
month. From that time forward I made it my business to
inquire, and in the stories which I am very fond of hearing
from all sorts and conditions of men, learned that in the time

of their distress it was always from the poor they sought assistance, and almost always from the poor they got it.

Trusting I have now satisfactorily answered your question, which I thank you for asking, I remain, with sincere compliments,

Robert Louis Stevenson.

X

Prayers

At Morning

The day returns and brings us the petty round of irritating concerns and duties. Help us to play the man, help us to perform them with laughter and kind faces, let cheerfulness abound with industry. Give us to go blithely on our business all this day, bring us to our resting beds weary and content and undishonoured, and grant us in the end the gift of sleep.

For Success

Lord, behold our family here assembled. We thank Thee for this place in which we dwell; for the love that unites us; for the peace accorded us this day; for the hope with which we expect the morrow; for the health, the work, the food, and the bright skies, that make our lives delightful; for our friends in all parts of the earth, and our friendly helpers in this foreign isle. Let peace abound in our small company. Purge out of every heart the lurking grudge. Give us grace and strength to forbear and to persevere. Offenders, give us the grace to accept and to forgive offenders. Forgetful ourselves, help us to bear cheerfully the forgetfulness of others. Give us courage and gaiety and the quiet mind. Spare to us our friends, soften to us our enemies. Bless us, if it may be, in all our innocent endeavours. If it may not, give us the strength to encounter that which is to come, that we be brave in peril, constant in tribulation, temperate in wrath, and in all changes of fortune, and down to the gates of death, loyal and loving one to another. As the clay to the potter, as the windmill to the wind, as children of their sire, we beseech of Thee this help and mercy for Christ's sake.

For Self Blame

LORD, enlighten us to see the beam that is in our own eye, and blind us to the mote that is in our brother's. Let us feel our offences with our hands, make them great and bright before us like the sun, make us eat them and drink them for our diet. Blind us to the offences of our beloved, cleanse them from our memories, take them out of our mouths for ever. Let all here before Thee carry and measure with the false balances of love, and be in their own eyes and in all conjunctures the most guilty. Help us at the same time with the grace of courage, that we be none of us cast down when we sit lamenting amid the ruins of our happiness or our integrity: touch us with fire from the altar, that we may be up and doing to rebuild our city; in the name and by the method of him in whose words of prayer we now conclude.

In Time of Rain

We thank Thee, Lord, for the glory of the late days and the excellent face of thy sun. We thank Thee for good news received. We thank Thee for the pleasures we have enjoyed and for those we have been able to confer. And now, when the clouds gather and the rain impends over the forest and our house, permit us not to be cast down; let us not lose the savour

of past mercies and past pleasures; but, like the voice of a bird
singing in the rain, let grateful memory survive in the hour of
darkness. If there be in front of us any painful duty, strengthen
us with the grace of courage; if any act of mercy, teach us
tenderness and patience.

For Renewal of Joy

We are evil, O God, and help us to see it and amend. We are
good, and help us to be better. Look down upon thy servants
with a patient eye, even as Thou sendest sun and rain; look
down, call upon the dry bones, quicken, enliven; re-create in
us the soul of service, the spirit of peace; renew in us the sense
of joy.